Mindfulness for Beginners

Practicing Minimalism and Meditation to Declutter Your Mind for Stress and Anxiety Relief

An Introduction to Mind Hacking Secrets in Plain English

Written by Jon Goldstein

© **Copyright 2018 by Jon Goldstein - All rights reserved.**

The following eBook is reproduced below with the goal of providing information that is as accurate and reliable as possible. Regardless, purchasing this eBook can be seen as consent to the fact that both the publisher and the author of this book are in no way experts on the topics discussed within and that any recommendations or suggestions that are made herein are for entertainment purposes only. Professionals should be consulted as needed prior to undertaking any of the action endorsed herein.

This declaration is deemed fair and valid by both the American Bar Association and the Committee of Publishers Association and is legally binding throughout the United States.

Furthermore, the transmission, duplication or reproduction of any of the following work including specific information will be considered an illegal act irrespective of if it is done electronically or in print. This extends to creating a secondary or tertiary copy of the work or a recorded copy and is only allowed with an expressed written consent from the Publisher. All additional rights reserved.

The information in the following pages is broadly considered to be a truthful and accurate account of facts and as such any inattention, use or misuse of the information in question by the reader will render any resulting actions solely under their purview. There are no scenarios in which the publisher or the original author of this work can be in any fashion deemed liable for any hardship or damages that may befall them after undertaking information described herein.

Additionally, the information in the following pages is intended only for informational purposes and should thus be thought of as universal. As befitting its nature, it is presented without assurance regarding its prolonged validity or interim quality. Trademarks that are mentioned are done without written consent and can in no

Jon Goldstein

way be considered an endorsement from the trademark holder.

Mindfulness for Beginners
Table of Contents

Introduction 6

Chapter 1: What Is Mindfulness, Exactly? 9

Chapter 2: The People of Mindfulness 22

Chapter 3: Essentialism vs. Minimalism vs. Meditation 39

Chapter 4: Let's Practice 51

Chapter 5: Daily Lives of Mindfulness 74

Chapter 6: The Fruits of No Labor 86

Chapter 7: No Risk, No Reward 102

Chapter 8: Answering Your Questions 109

Chapter 9: A Little More About a Little Less 116

Chapter 10: Mindfulness-Based Stress Reduction 127

Conclusion 153

Jon Goldstein
Introduction

The world we inhabit today is filled to the brim with dark energy, and though you may not believe it, there is a part of you that knows it is the truth. The age of technology has opened us in so many wonderful ways—to communication, knowledge, and all the wonderful things the World Wide Web has to offer. But alongside this, society has also opened itself up to an ongoing rush of negative opinions, catty fights, and poor political decisions made by the 1% who don't stop to think how their words and actions affect the other 99%.

Anxiety and stress have always existed among mankind, and it has always been one of our most pervasive illnesses. It only appears more common nowadays, because now people are no longer afraid to voice it. No longer do we live in an age where you keep your problems boxed into yourself, silently shouldering these burdens because, as they say, "Someone else has it worse." Yes, it's true; someone else does have it worse.

But this doesn't mean you have to live with your problems.

Like darkness, stress is something that feeds on itself. It pulls you down, and you lash your bad moods out at others, who send you more negative emotions in return. It's a vicious cycle, one that only continues to be fed by the news you see on your phone every morning; more unfortunate events and natural disasters tempered by inane celebrity distractions.

But what if there was a way to break the wheel? A way to remove the stress and anxiety from your mind. As it turns out, there is, and more and more people have been turning to it to free their mind against the incoming, nonstop turmoil that is life. It's called mindfulness, and you may be surprised to hear it's been around since the 1970s.

Mindfulness, paired with the offshoot practices of essentialism and minimalism, are developed psychiatric techniques that stemmed from Buddhism but have evolved into something beyond religion. Used to treat anxiety, addiction, and even behavioral problems in children, mindfulness is a technique that can help everyone in the certain ways they need it.

In the following pages, you will find everything you have ever wanted, or needed, to know about mindfulness. What it is? How to use it? How not to use it? What is essentialism, you wonder, and how does that differ from minimalism? How is either of those things different from mindfulness? What do any of these words even mean? Whatever questions you have, we are here to answer them. By the time you have reached the conclusion, you will be more than ready to start a new chapter of your life. A new you, untouched by the darkness creeping on the edges of our modern world.

The great part is, you don't even need a new year to start.

Chapter 1: What Is Mindfulness, Exactly?

Very rarely can you look at a term and explain it as, "Well, it's exactly what it sounds like." Primarily, mindfulness doesn't really sound like anything, so you might be left on a bit of a blank. Secondly, further introspection will only confuse you further. Does it mean that you are mindful of everything you do? Or that your mind is full of things, all the time?

To make things even more complicated, here's the answer: is it both, and neither.

When you breathe, you breathe automatically. But if someone says to you, "Are you breathing?" Your body's response is to put itself on manual breathing. Now, you are paying attention to every movement your lungs make. As they open, you feel the air moving down and into them, the oxygen seeping into your bloodstream and carrying to your brain. Your brain, telling your lungs to exhale and send the carbon dioxide back out. Maybe you're one of these people, who only get three-quarters of the way through an exhale before you breathe back in, or perhaps you need to get every last thing out, and maybe you wait a moment with empty lungs, before breathing in again. There—you're thinking about it now.

That, in the simplest of terms, is mindfulness. You are bringing yourself to the here and now, centering yourself in the present. Every action that you make has a specific reason, and you think about everything you do, as you do it. So, are you mindful of everything you do? Yes, you move with deliberation. Is your mind full of things? Yes, you're thinking of every action that you make, as you make it, and taking in the world around you on the whole.

But those are just the simple terms and an easy way to explain it to the uninitiated. If you've purchased this book, you're here for the full package. So let's take a closer look at the complicatedly simple concept of 'mindfulness.'

A History Lesson

Like most modern meditation and new-age philosophies, mindfulness began as a separate concept within the religion of Buddhism. The original Pali term, 'sati,' can also be translated as 'awareness.' You can see how the words 'mindful' and 'aware,' though not identical, echo one another in their intentions. It is one of the tenements of the Eightfold Path, a series of eight concepts practiced by Buddhists in order to achieve Nirvana.

But mindfulness, as we know, is not mired to Buddhism, or to any religion. The one to first take it and apply it to psychology was a man named Jon Kabat-Zinn.

The Man Named Kabat

Born in 1944, this American professor of molecular biology is the reason mindfulness first breached the minds of the Western public. During the time of the Vietnam War, Kabat-Zinn was in MIT and campaigned heavily, both against the war and against the military research going on. He has gone on record to say that this period of his life was his karmic awakening. He found his purpose in mindfulness, his mission to spread it out to the world.

A Zen missionary named Philip Kapleau had come to MIT and was teaching meditation to the students. There must have been something in what Kapleau taught because Kabat-Zinn was unable to let it go. He went on to study under other famous Buddhist teachers, perfecting his technique, and eventually, he brought it back to MIT.

When Kabat-Zinn brought his learned mindfulness to the world of scholars, he didn't present it as a faction of Buddhism. Instead, he approached it from a psychological angle. The eight-week program he implemented is still known today as Mindfulness-Based Stress Reduction, or MBSR. There is now an entire center within MIT that Kabat-Zinn founded, known as the Center for Mindfulness.

Kabat-Zinn has gone on to write a number of books on the subject, including some about parenting with his wife, Myla Zinn. He is by no means the only reigning voice on mindfulness, nor does he pretend to be. He is only a voice who first brought mindfulness into the public consciousness, and the first to apply it to a non-religious setting. In the years since then, mindfulness has expanded to become one of the most popular tactics of stress reduction and other voices have chimed in with their own history and experiences.

Doctor Davidson

Richard J. Davidson is another pioneer in the field of mental wellness. He is a psychologist who is known for working alongside the Dalai Lama, learning his teachings and bringing them back to the field of psychology. Currently, he is the founder and chair of the Center for Healthy Minds.

Davidson brought an interesting new angle to the plate, where he talks about the plasticity of the brain. Happiness and compassion, argues Davidson, are like any skill. And like any skill, they can be taught. This confuses many, many people upon first notice because aren't happiness and compassion things that people intrinsically know? Well, perhaps the baseline emotion of love is. But thinking about it, happiness and compassion are two things that you can find yourself sorely lacking. It's not so much about you not putting the work in, however, and more about these things slipping out of your grasp due to outside circumstances. Davidson's argument is that you can reach out and grab those things by teaching your brain to be happy.

Davidson's own practices have also changed with time, as he has spent so much time with meditation that his personal philosophies change. Because of this, he now postulates that meditation actually changes your brain, as well as your body. He teaches now for the benefit of others, and not for the benefit of his own research.

Though Davidson does not often use mindfulness specifically, we can see echoes of it throughout his work. He is an intelligent man who has learned from the best, and it is clear from his own experiences that he has touched on some kind of universal truth. Just because happiness is hard for you to reach the moment, that doesn't mean you can't teach yourself happiness. Can it really be as simple as 'I tell myself to be happy, so I am happy?' Sometimes, fake it until you make it.

The Pollyanna Principle

Back in 1913, the novel Pollyanna was written. The titular protagonist of the story was a girl who played something called "the glad game"— meaning that in every situation she found herself in, she looked for something to be happy about.

There exists something known as a positivity bias, meaning that your brain focuses more on happy memories than sad ones. This creates an outlook on the past that romanticizes it, making it feel better than it really was. While it is postulated that the common percentage of humans have this positivity bias, this is not true of people who suffer from anxiety or depression in any form of the word. Pessimists, negative outlooks, and depressive realists are far more likely to see the world in an unflattering bias.

While the terms "positivity bias" and "Pollyanna Principle" are often used interchangeably, there is a leeway. For the sake of applying it to mindfulness, you can split them into two separate paths; looking back and looking forward. Positivity bias, similarly to nostalgia goggles, is all about seeing the good in the past and remembering it to be better than it was. It is not that positivity bias is a bad thing, as your brain is always happy to draw on positive memories. But it's not as helpful when it comes to training your brain for happiness.

The Pollyanna Principle, on the other hand, can be seen as a way of looking forward. Play the glad game with yourself. Always find something to be happy about, no matter the situation you find yourself in. This can begin to train your brain to look for the positives, subconsciously urging you to seek out happiness throughout your daily life.

You can see how a variety of research on different topics can come under the domain of mindfulness, as it is used in tandem with a range of different techniques. This is because, right from the start, mindfulness itself had different influences urging it on in various directions.

The Edge of Hinduism

Though mindfulness in its full name does not appear as one of the tenements of Hinduism, the concept is rooted all throughout the religion. This is most notably through meditation and yoga. Both these practices focus on centering the mind and calming yourself. It is no surprise that both are taught as a part of mindfulness.

For many who practice yoga, it's just about the exercise. And it is good stretching, but yoga was not built on those principles. Rather, the various 'poses' set up in yoga are meant to stimulate your spirituality. So when using yoga in mindfulness, your goal is not only to stretch out your muscles but also to train your mind. Remember how Davidson believed the brain could be taught happiness? The existence of endorphins when it comes to exercise is no doubt a small part of how yoga can be used as a method for this.

Other Influences

It has been noted that mindfulness, in the way we learn it today, was not only inspired by Buddhism and Hinduism but by other religions worldwide such as Judaism and Islam. This is a double-edged sword of truth. There are plenty of religions—indeed, even non-religious groups—that have practiced mindfulness over the last few millennia. However, it was brought to attention by the modern, Western world, from these Buddhist roots.

Pointing out the widespread historical usage of mindfulness does less to argue about the development of it and more to prove that it just works. Like meditation which was similarly practiced in ancient Rome. Nobody who meditates does it because they read about the

Romans doing it. It always comes from Buddhism and Hinduism and other 'enlightened' sources from the hippie era. That doesn't change the fact that the Romans meditated. It only proves that meditation works.

Enlightenment

This is a term that gets thrown around by everyone from scientists to new age incense burners looking to open their third eye, so it can be hard to find a textbook definition. But the truth is, enlightenment varies on a person-to-person basis and what it means for you and your beliefs might be different from everyone else. One of the outcomes of mindfulness is to achieve enlightenment on this personal level, and it means that you will better understand yourself and your place in the world.

One of the great misconceptions held by the world at large is that we use only ten percent of our brain power. Despite scientists reminding us multiple times that this simply isn't true, year after year we see film and TV using it as a plot point. So why does this concept keep popping up, despite all arguments telling that it isn't real? Because, while the brain power bit is not true; the bit about the ten percent actually is. It is not so much about using our brain power, as it is being present in the moment. At any given time of the day, we are only living about ten percent in the present. Our minds are constantly thinking of other things—planning out the rest of our week; thinking about the future; hung up on something that happened in the past; wondering what your friends are doing and winning arguments against the people we don't like.

The main goal behind practicing mindfulness is to get rid of all the excess going on inside your head. Through lots of practice and daily meditation, you can bring your mind from ten percent to fifty percent, and eventually completely into the present.

So now, we circle back to our first point. Mindfulness is at once complicated and simple. Is it being mindful of all things? Yes. Pay attention to everything you do and every choice you make. Deliberation is the key. But it is not as simple as saying you think extra hard about everything you do. Is your mind full of things? Yes, full of the present. But it is also emptied of anything unnecessary bogging you down. You are aware, but not hyperaware.

Everyone has a different definition of what mindfulness means, from different dictionary definitions to the meaning outlined by pioneers and practitioners themselves. Don't be afraid to let it take on a new meaning for you, either.

Jon Goldstein
Chapter 2: The People of Mindfulness

While researching mindfulness, the history, and the practices, you may find yourself wondering, is this really right for me? Am I the right sort of person to practice mindfulness? Maybe the problems specific to you aren't the kind of problems that can be normally dealt with using the mindfulness technique. Or, maybe your problems are wide, vast and unspecified, and mindfulness is too specific for such a broad range. Perhaps you're thinking that, whatever has been plaguing you, it is too serious and runs too deep for mindfulness to ever really make a dent. Or, on the flip side, your problems are shallow and not nearly as serious as what others struggle with daily. There are a hundred ways to rationalize it away, thinking that mindfulness is right for someone else, but not you.

Well, let us dig into it. Who are the people of mindfulness? Are you the right sort of person to practice it? In this chapter, we aim to find out.

Anxiety

Of course, dealing with anxiety is one of the driving factors behind mindfulness. Along with its brother, stress; anxiety is an incredibly common illness facing the population at large. Now, there are several ways anxiety presents itself in the human brain. The first is through anxiety disorders, a grouping of mental disorders that cause panic and extreme fear in the patient. It's a fear of the future combined with a fear of present events, and symptoms range from shaking to regular panic attacks wherein the sufferer shuts down completely.

There aren't a lot of medication options open for those with anxiety disorder. Sometimes pills such as antidepressants will be prescribed to help improve symptoms, but this is in no way a guarantee that anything will happen. More often, anxiety is dealt with through lifestyle change or cognitive therapy. And, as with prescribed medication, there's honestly no guarantee that those will work either. But it is generally agreed to be the best path.

Instead of paying for a therapist or a lifestyle coach, more and more with an anxiety disorder are turning to mindfulness.

More common throughout the wider population is a high-stress level, and symptoms of anxiety manifest within people not diagnosed with the disorder. Social anxiety has become the favorite diagnosis of the young generation, and it's not all that wrong—for the technological age that we live in, social interactions have become difficult for young adults, and social anxiety is the best description of how many feel. For those with these symptoms, it's often touted that it is not as bad as 'real anxiety,' and the only advice given is really to suck it up. But if your symptoms of stress are casual and not related to the full-blown disorder, that's just as valid a reason to practice mindfulness. No one should ever tell you that your experiences are not valid, and no one's way of dealing with their issues should ever be to just 'suck it up.'

Depression

Much like anxiety, there are two kinds of sufferers when it comes to depression; those with diagnosed depression, and those who exhibit casual symptoms. These can be things like sleeping too much and losing interest in your hobbies, but can also include much more serious threats such as self-harm or worse.

While mindfulness is not a proven tactic to help combat clinical depression, it is recommended to try. No harm can come from you looking for a positive viewpoint. And for those who exhibit symptoms without the diagnosis, there's a very good chance this depressive fugue is due to the uncertainty of our future. Taking up mindfulness is a way to cope with this fear, just as it does for stress.

Jon Goldstein
Dealing with Children

This is the same for those who are parents, and those who work with children. Mindfulness isn't just a way to deal with the natural stress of looking after children. It can also be a handy tool in teaching better behavior. Especially when it comes to very young children when naptime is already a part of their daily routine, you can encourage a kind of meditation to add before sleeping to calm them down. While very young children won't grasp the difficult concepts, of course, you can encourage quiet time, where everyone in the room sits with their eyes closed and thinks about things.

Psychologists have begun to consider using mindfulness as a way to deal with aggressive behavior in children. This behavior usually stems from two sources. Either the child is naturally unruly, or they have an underlying mental disorder. Children are susceptible to anything to ADHD, separation anxiety, or another kind of disorder known as Oppositional Defiant Disorder. While it can be hard to diagnose children, you can start to use mindfulness to help improve behavior no matter the underlying cause.

Have a kid sit down, and play with some kind of stimulus—something like squeezable sand or goo, found in any local toy store—and really pay attention to every detail. If it is easier for the child, they can recite back to you out loud everything that they feel. This first little introduction to mindfulness is a gateway to finding coping behaviors, relaxation, and introspection into their own thoughts. Mindfulness is a consideration of all things, and you can easily steer that consideration to other people's feelings.

If you have children or work with children, give mindfulness a try as a group. Children are always more receptive to things everyone can do together, so if you do it alongside them, they will be much more likely to really sit with you and learn it properly. Adjust the amount you teach to the child's age and their learning capabilities.

Substance Abuse

There's nothing wrong with admitting it. If you have an addiction and you want to quit it, trying new techniques to make yourself better is worth praising. And if you are going to go in any direction, mindfulness is an excellent choice. Doctors have already noted how effective mindfulness can be in fighting addiction whether your vice is drugs, alcohol, cigarettes, or a combination, whatever you've grown to find yourself relying on and want to let go of.

Clinical Disorders

There's a variety of mental disorders that run alongside anxiety, from bipolar to psychosis to Borderline Personality Disorder. The negative connotations with these words alone have led to patients pulling away from society, cutting off from friend and family, and other possible healthy relationships. It is hard to make friends or hold down a job due to the automatic reactions you face, and opening up to anyone seems out of the picture.

Mindfulness has become part of therapy sessions for people with mental disorders. But the wonderful thing about mindfulness is that you don't need someone to guide you through it. You don't even need to leave your house. For those who are working with psychiatrists, the results have been very positive. Some looking to the future have even hypothesized that mindfulness can help prevent the development of such mental disorders. Though unproven, it certainly is not harmful to try. If certain disorders run in your family and you find yourself in a constant state of worry that you'll one day inherit them, try mindfulness as a way to work against it. Shield your psyche, if you will.

Millennial

It's a common joke going around the Internet to say, "The millennials are killing X industry!" But all joking aside, it's more accurate to say, "The millennials are killing themselves." And often in a literal sense, but mostly we see almost every young person is struggling with these feelings of being dead inside. Monotony has always been a problem, but in the past, the main way to fight against it was with hope. Working towards a brighter future made it easier to put in work hours and save money for that college tuition and dream house. But now, the young people of the world don't see a bright future ahead of them. All anyone sees is a broken economy, a corrupt class system, and a job that won't even cover half an apartment's rent, let alone a house for a family. The cultural zeitgeist consists of half-hearted, cutting jokes about depression and the pain that seems to just come with being a millennial.

Instead of living with the pain, because it doesn't seem that the world is going to drastically change anytime soon, try using mindfulness as a way to find your personal happiness. Think of it as a boat out on stormy waters, or an island to build a shelter on. Maybe the future does look dark and grim, but with a light in your hands, maybe you can be the one to start the ball rolling towards a possible better future.

A Recent Break-Up

The ending of a long-term relationship that was a cornerstone of your personal life can be a thousand times more heartbreaking if you are already under pressure from the stress of other things in your life. This could be a divorce which was coming for a long time but you thought perhaps you could work it out. It could be a future with someone, ripped from your hands and left you with no idea where to go from here. It doesn't even need to be the end of a romantic relationship. Friendships can end irrevocably, leaving you without a piece of your support system. And don't think that this only applies to relationships that were ended by the other party, either. Sometimes you were the one to end it. Sometimes, even though you know it was the right thing to do, it can leave you feeling empty and questioning your decisions.

There are several reasons why mindfulness can help through a situation like this. Point one is, as always, the stress. If you are already suffering from an outside problem, the added weight of this ended relationship is not going to make things any better. You can also very easily start circling down a drain, wondering if you've made the right call after all. Sometimes, just the heartbreak itself is enough of a reason.

In situations like this, mindfulness isn't just a way to deal with stress. It also gives you something else to focus your energy on. Mindfulness is a lot of things, but important to this scenario is that it does not allow for wallowing. Use it as a vehicle to stop your heart from getting overwhelmed with the sadness that comes with this ending.

Family Matters

Living with your family can prove itself to be simultaneously a blessing and a curse. But the scales can be tipped in favor of either blessing or curse, depending on what your family life is like.

Parents are kind, but they can also be overwhelming. Living under the same roof as people from whom you suffer constant scrutiny is not good for your mental health, and no matter how many times you try to explain that hovering over your shoulder and asking questions about the future is not helpful, parents will continue to do it anyway. The frustration that wells up inside as a side effect of being put under that constant pressure causes you to lash out and fights can break out often. Use mindfulness as a way to set yourself apart. Distance can be a good thing, even from the people we love. Daily meditation will help you control that frustration, and even if you still have no answers about your future, you will be able to have a conversation about it without snapping or starting an argument. Mindfulness has also been proven to teach the users how to be mindful of the feelings of others, and so you can use it to understand your parent's perspective a little more. Remember that they care so much because they love you. Be mindful of the things you have in your life to be grateful for, and when you feel those frustrations bubbling up again, use your mindfulness to change the mood.

But it is a sad truth of the world we live in that not all parents are so well-meaning. Difficult family situations range from roughly trying to scrape by financially, to suffering abuse at the hands of your relatives. One of the hardest parts of living in a situation like that is sometimes you are unable to leave. A variety of factors can contribute to a person being stuck in a situation where they are not safe in their own home. While there are many resources you can reach out to if you are living with people who do not put your safety and happiness first, using mindfulness and meditation is one of those resources. The practice can assure you that you are here, that you are alive, and you matter. Your voice matters, your happiness matters, and your opinions matter. Most importantly, you have a place in the universe. With mindfulness as a base, you can begin seeking the outside help you need.

Police Academy

Yes, mindfulness is recommended for anyone involved in law enforcement, and it shouldn't be hard to see why. Police officers in today's society are under more scrutiny than ever before, and for good reason. What good is it, if the people meant to be upholding the law, are lawless themselves?

But there are so many deeper issues at play that come with police work, and mindfulness can help adapt to these problems and solve them in the best way possible.

Mindfulness, living in the present moment, can keep an officer safe during active duty. This same sentiment goes for anyone working in a high-risk profession, where life rests on being able to make split-second decisions. A mindful person is better equipped to make these decisions and knows the right one to choose without hesitation. If mindfulness was implemented as part of training, there would be a decrease in their poor decisions made by officers on the spot. A single one within law enforcement practicing mindfulness still makes a difference.

Apart from the decisions, a benefit of being mindful is within the changing perceptions of others. Two common problems facing people outside of law enforcement are racial profiling and underlying grudges. While profiling is a common part of chasing criminals, too often race is brought into that profile. Harmful stereotypes lead to people of certain ethnicities, most commonly Middle Eastern or African-American, being treated differently by the law system for no reason other than the color of their skin.

One of the first practices learned in mindfulness is the ability to separate ourselves from our emotions. If more officers practiced mindfulness like this, they could separate themselves from their prejudices, and learn to see all human beings as equal. While some are racist on purpose, there are always those who spout casual racism, the general public who don't even realize that the things they say, and the way they act, affects people of a different race, gender, or sexuality. Mindfulness will bring out that awareness in someone, and while of course, this is always an important part of being human, for those who work within the police force it will more greatly affect the others around.

Anyone who currently works in law enforcement knows the pressure you are under every day. Any wrong judgment call will be scrutinized by the entire nation, the entire world, even. Practicing mindfulness brings you to be the best judge in character you can be, and you will be sound and solid that the decisions you make are right—even if you have less than a second to make it.

I Am Bored

Is this a valid reason for taking up mindfulness? Yes, of course, it is. Because of its use in therapy, mindfulness goes hand in hand with such heavy topics as previously discussed. But mindfulness does not discriminate who practices within its teachings. You don't need to have any deeper reasons for it, other than you are bored, or curious. If you just want to try it for the sake of trying it, by all means, you are more than welcome.

In conclusion, the short answer to the question is yes. Yes, you are the right kind of person to practice mindfulness. You, with your own specific set of stressors, your unique faults, and your particular living habits. The answer is always yes.

Mindfulness is tied to no religion and is born from no organization. There is no rulebook stating who is and isn't allowed to participate. It exists only to help you feel better, you the individual, more at ease with yourself.

The wonderful thing about the world we live in today is that people are becoming less and less afraid of asking for help. Going to therapy is no longer a social stigma, and so many are applauded by friends and family for seeking the help they need. Knowing that mindfulness is right for you, don't be afraid to start immediately.

So now that you know mindfulness is right for you, let's explore.

Chapter 3: Essentialism vs. Minimalism vs. Meditation

When it comes to the smaller terms associated with mindfulness, it is easier to think of mindfulness itself as the umbrella and let the other terms fall underneath it. The biggest of these three sub-terms are essentialism, minimalism, and meditation. We've already talked a little about meditation, but the other two might sound new. Moreover, they sound a little similar. We're going into a bit of a deep dive into the differences between all these three sub-terms, and how they relate to mindfulness as a whole.

Essentialism, Then

Don't mistake this term as meaning 'the essentials.' The root actually comes from Plato's philosophy that all living things have an essence.

The idea behind essentialism is that every living thing has two states: matter, and form. The matter is the solid bits that make you up, like blood and flesh and bone. Form, or essence, can be likened to the spirit or soul. For Plato, the universe was essentially perfect and anything that humans saw that could be perceived as imperfections were just that, perceptions. We are not able to truly see the essence, and Plato went on to describe this by stating that a perfect circle exists, but one cannot draw it without some flaw. Artists promptly spent the next the next 2,000 years learning to draw a perfect circle.

The important takeaway from Plato's musings about the essence is that human eyes have a limited perception. Things are good, and right, and the way they were always meant to be. It's only that we, as a species, can't perceive that version of reality and so we are faced with the imperfections. Not being able to trust in the essence of the world can be a huge stressor in our lives, and one of the main reasons why we begin to feel so lost and without purpose or direction.

Psychological essentialism has grown away from Plato's original concept, as tends to happen with old Greek philosophies. It relates less to the world as a whole, and instead focuses more on the essence of the individual. Again, take us back to the concept of the soul. This form of essentialism states that there is something more that drives our behavior, more than simple electrical impulses and synapses firing in the brain.

But psychology takes it a step further, postulating that the essence of certain things has been so permeated into the way we look at the world that certain concepts have an 'essence' already attached to them. It has even been argued that this perceived essence of things is what leads to stereotypes, as old world beliefs that certain groups of people all share the same kind of 'essence' that predisposes them to be a certain way.

Understand it a little bit better? Honestly, it's fine if you don't. Philosophy is a big topic and comes with so much thought and change over the years, even students of philosophy struggle with the concepts. The thing about it is it's a mindset.

That's the key. It's a way of looking at the world and of changing our perceptions. And how does it relate to mindfulness? Be mindful of the way you perceive the world around you. Remember that its true nature may not be the way you've seen it. Pay attention.

Essentialism, Now

And now that you have a bit of a better understanding of essentialism, get ready to learn an entirely new mindset! In recent years, a new offshoot of essentialism has taken root, and it has surprisingly little to do with all the previous thousands of years' worth of pondering on the subject. Instead, the modern outlook takes the other root word and boils it down to 'the essentials.' Just like the old essentialism didn't do.

The modern movement of essentialism involves shaving off the things in your life that you don't need. This new take has much more to do with mindfulness than the old way does, and in fact, was likely born from the same place. You can see the same basic concepts present in Buddhism rooted here in essentialism. But instead of looking at the Buddhist path of mindfulness in broad strokes, essentialism instead takes concept and hyper-focus in on it.

One of the precepts of Buddhism is that material gain and wealth are only present in this lifetime, and forming such attachments will weight you down and prevent you from achieving Nirvana.

This new form of essentialism was introduced to the world mainly through author Greg McKeown, whose book "Essentialism: The Disciplined Pursuit of Less" had one purpose to state to the world: do less, so you can accomplish more. It's the same principle all your teachers taught you in school which is quality over quantity.

It's a fair idea, that we stretch ourselves too thin by trying too many different things. Part of this always falls back on that old adage, that there simply aren't enough hours in a day to do everything we need, and so we cram it all in. Essentialism urges you to take a step back, and maybe realize that we don't need to do all these things. This mostly applies to work or school life.

Think of a college student, cramming for five final exams within one week. It's an image everyone knows all too well—staying up all night to study, on a desk covered with note paper, drinking far too many cups of caffeine. Realistically, how good are these grades going to be? Instead of focusing their energy on one subject to really let themselves learn and absorb the information, they have pulled themselves in five different directions and the pool of knowledge remains shallow. Not only will they not do as well in the exam, but it is likely that this information will fade away due to not being fully ingrained in the student's mind.

How do you process your work? If you have a job, take yourself through a day. Are you really committing yourself to a single task? Or do you find yourself running around, jumping from one thing to the next without really ever finishing the previous task properly? One common problem faced by younger or a newcomer at work, especially those in lower positions of power, is that they tend to be used as gophers. Every person who walks by has something they need you to do, some errand to run, some small thing to fix. A boss might have a constant stream of orders coming down. Do this, do that, no, finish this first, but remember to do that next, and then this other thing. It can't be hard to see how this affects your output, not to mention your mentality.

Teachers have begun to implement this new wave of essentialism in their programs, from kindergarten through high school. Some have chosen to abstain from homework. As has been pointed out, even if it is only half an hour's worth of work, half an hour from six subjects is three hours' worth of work. Combined with the new requirements for daily physical activity and a young brain's need for proper rest, it is no wonder so many kids struggle in school. So homework is forgone and replaced with in-class work, where teachers hope to take a more hands-on approach. Several school systems have begun to eliminate standardized tests from their curriculum as well, because of the aforementioned problems that arise from having too many tests. These are ways of adapting essentialism into our lives, making us work harder and better.

Obviously, this new essentialism isn't much similar to the old essentialism, and really, they should have two different names. But using them both in your pursuit of mindfulness is important.

Minimalism

Now, this one might set you back a step. Because minimalism, as most of us know it, isn't a kind of philosophy or psychology or other religious-based practice—it's an art form. A stylistic interpretation that involves removing all the clutter and keeping the canvas as blank and plain as you possibly can. Ah, you may be starting to get the picture.

Practicing minimalism in your daily life is all about taking out the extra clutter. Clean out the garbage in your attic, if you will. More is less, and less is more. It's a common knowledge among those who suffer from short attention spans that a clean workspace helps your output.

If you observe the way architecture has changed over the last hundred years, you can see how minimalism is making a large mark on the landscape. While it is true that styles throughout history like to repeat themselves, going from classic to overcrowded to classic again, minimalism has taken off in recent years like never before. And it can be argued that this kind of architecture has become so popular due to a collective subconscious desire: we all want things to be simpler. We want our buildings to look on the outside how we wish we felt on the inside. Clean, simple, and without all the fuss.

Minimalism and the new wave of essentialism are very similar concepts, but they are not one and the same. Think of it as being the difference between inside and outside. Essentialism in inside your own head and minimalism is outside of it. In essentialism, we are stripping down the tasks that we do. But in minimalism, we strip down the world around us. Both of these principles feed off of one another and both are a large part of practicing mindfulness. However, neither are necessary steps. While you can adopt some pieces from essentialism or minimalism to suit your lifestyle, if you don't think that they are for you, you don't need to adhere to both.

Meditation

There are many ways to practice meditation, but there is one way in particular that one should focus on in regards to mindfulness. See, we get our word from the Latin 'meditatio', meaning 'to think.' That was how the Romans did their meditation. Instead of calming and completely emptying the mind, they would sit and think for hours on end. Pondering the meaning of life like a college student, or someone trapped in an office job with no desire to be there, staring blankly at their computer screen for hours on end.

This is closer to the particular kind of meditation that is associated with mindfulness. Through translations in some ancient texts, the word 'meditation' is seen as interchangeable with 'contemplation.' And contemplation is a very good word to go hand in hand with mindfulness.

Unlike essentialism or minimalism, meditation is a necessary part of practicing mindfulness. It is one of the foundry blocks, a basis for which all other exercises are built on. Rather than taking what you need to suit your lifestyle and using it in such a particular way, meditation is a solid to fall back on. A rulebook, if you will. However, many mindfulness centers will use the two terms interchangeably. They are not the same. Meditation is something that you take time out of your day to do and involves sitting in one place and focusing your mind on certain things. Mindfulness proper is a state of mind that you aim to be in all the time, not something you set yourself up for every day.

And those are the differences between the under-umbrella terms. As you go forward and learn how to practice mindfulness, you can see how bits and pieces of essentialism and minimalism float through. With this knowledge under your belt, you are ready to start learning the exercises involved in mindfulness.

Chapter 4: Let's Practice

So you want to start practicing mindfulness right away? Fair enough, but be aware that it won't be an easy change to make immediately. While it sounds simple enough on the surface, this is something regular practitioners have been training in for years. It is not as simple as deciding to 'make yourself aware.'

Before getting started, remember that there are different levels to which you can devote yourself to mindfulness, and any level of dedication is perfectly fine. For some, practicing mindfulness is a short exercise to do daily, as a walk around the block. People like this are not necessarily looking for a change in mindset, just a way to clear out their personal cobwebs every day so nothing gets piled up too high. For others, the end goal is to fully immerse themselves in mindfulness. Like Dr. Davidson, whose entire outlook and lifestyle changed because of his meditative practices, these people are looking for a completely different road to drive themselves down. And you, personally, may find yourself falling anywhere between the scale.

Don't think that you have to have it figured out before you start. It's quite all right to not know what you want, to decide in the middle of the process, or to change your mind partway through. As you learn the practices, decide for yourself just how much time and effort you feel you need to put in. Never feel pressured to do any more or less than what makes you feel comfortable.

Cleaning

Cleaning isn't so much a practice as it is a preparation. Clearing out a physical space is a way to visualize mindfulness and the way we use it to clean our minds.

- ❖ Choose the space you want to clean. It's most effective when this place is where you plan to do most of your meditation. Sometimes this is a living room or a den, but more often than not it is your own bedroom.

- ❖ Section the room off. A messy room is overwhelming to look at because the big picture seems like it's just too much to handle, and then you find you can't even start. Instead, looking at the space in small sections keeps it manageable and keeps you focused on one thing at a time. When making a goal chart, always start small.

- ❖ First, clean the room on a surface level. Section by section, make the floor clear. Empty the surfaces. As you do, think about each article that you pick up. What is it, why do you have it, where do you want it to go?

- ❖ Don't be afraid to throw things away. Attachments to things that we never use are what cause a good portion of messes in the first place. Keep a bin near the door. As you pick up each article, consider whether you truly need it. Sometimes things are for the garbage, and other times you can donate to others in need. Clothes, furniture, old toys, there are plenty of things you might have found yourself too attached to that you don't actually need. Let go.

❖ Once the surface cleaning is done, go deeper. Again, do this in sections. Organize all your drawers. It can be amazing, the number of things hidden away in the far corners of cabinets that you had completely forgotten about. Consider why these things are hidden in a drawer. Is it for practicality? Or had you forgotten about their existence so much, that if you tossed it in the bin, you would never think of it again?

❖ After that comes the cleaning of the walls and floors. While cleaning floors is common, plenty of people forget to wipe down their walls. In your cleaning, take a rag and some disinfectant and scrub at the walls and the doors. Wipe down the light fixtures and the legs on your desk, if you have one.

- ❖ Don't forget about the windows. Clean the glass and the attached coverings. Vacuum curtains and wipe down blinds.
- ❖ If you're the kind of person who likes it, light a scented candle or burn some sage when you've finished.

Depending on the size of the room and how messy it was, to begin with, this is a process that can take all day. But locking yourself up and dedicating a day to the cleansing of a room can be an incredibly fulfilling way to spend your Saturday. While it may be tempting to invite a friend to join you, this is a distraction. Your room will get clean, but you won't get the experience of visualizing mindfulness as you would alone.

See, the meticulous way the room was sectioned off and cleaned piece by piece is a representation of the way our brain works when we practice mindfulness. It is the deliberate movement and consideration of all things as we do them one by one. And on top of everything, now not only do you have visualization—you have a safe space for meditation.

Mindfulness Meditation

The phrase 'safe space' can be thrown around too carelessly and the true importance behind it has gotten reduced to something of an online joke. The original purpose of a safe space is not to have the entire world safe for you, but to have one specific place you know you can go to alleviate tension.

Having a space like this is needed not just for mindfulness, but for all forms of meditation. The practice involves a complete relaxation of your body, and you can't accomplish that when you don't feel comfortable in the space you are in. Do some preparations beforehand to make sure everything about the place you plan to meditate in is as comfortable as it can be. Burning scented candles or sage can make the room smell just the way you want it to. Control the temperature with your thermostat. Have it be uncluttered, so you don't find yourself distracted by anything around you. Wherever you choose to sit or lie, make sure it's comfortable. Put some cushions on the floor, or angle a chair just right, or lie on your bed with your feet elevated.

When starting meditation, parties recommend that you begin with a ten-minute interval per day. As you find yourself getting more and more comfortable in the process, you can add more time, you can do it multiple times a day, for as long as you feel you need. If you are an early bird, then do it for ten minutes after you wake up in the morning. Allow your mind to be clean and positive as you face the day. If you are not a morning person at all and tend to do things more in the evening, use meditation as a way to wind down before bed. In order to keep yourself to a ten-minute segment, set an alarm before you start.

Once you are fully comfortable and set in your space, begin to meditate. There are two ways you can choose to accomplish mindfulness meditation; either through guided meditation or on your own. For more information on the different kinds of meditation to pick up and how to truly master it, check out the companion book "Meditation for Beginners: The Leading Guide on How to Practice Transcendental Meditation for Anxiety and Stress Relief, Weight Loss, Sleep, Healing, Happiness, and Mindfulness."

Listen Up

One of the head definitions of mindfulness is to be mindful of others. Think back to the last conversation you had with someone. Did you really fully listen to what they had to say, every time they opened their mouth? Don't feel bad if you didn't. It's part of human nature to tune people out, even accidentally. The conversation may remind you of something else and your brain might go off on a tangent. Plenty of people find themselves overthinking what they plan on saying next, running the same sentence in their head multiple times before saying it and completely missing what your conversational partner had been getting at.

There is more than one way to learn mindfulness through the art of listening. Most prominent of these is by listening to others. This is a very good excuse to reconnect with old friends and have those relationships grow strong again, something that's beneficial for the well-being of your mind. You can have these conversations with people either by technology, say over the phone or through video chatting software, or you can meet up with someone and talk face to face. The only way to avoid conversation is through a text or messaging software. In order to complete this exercise, you need to be able to hear someone's voice.

When listening to someone in a mindful way, you are doing more than just listening at the surface level. Take in every word they say. Let it sink in before you give your response. In fact, try not to give any responses at all, unless prompted. Listening mindfully is just about that—listening. Don't attempt to turn the conversation in a certain direction, and don't try to make it about yourself in any way. Let your partner steer the direction, have them talk about anything and everything they want.

As you listen, take into account every minor shift and inflection of their voice. Fully listening means you aren't just hearing the words, but everything that comes along with them. Things like the breathiness of someone's voice, how much air comes out with every word, and whether it passes more through their nose, or their mouth. Do you find them nasal, or are they someone who speaks from the chest? Does their voice sit low in the back of their throat? Do they have any kind of an accent, is it pronounced, or is it so vague that you can only hear it on certain words? There are so many nuances to the way people talk, things that we never pick up on because our focus is not fully trained on the speaker. There are even little things such as the way someone ends a sentence. Some people have a cadence that raises the ends of a sentence into a question, even if it was not a question being spoken. You will be surprised at how many things you notice when you really pay attention.

More than the voice, too, is someone's face. While seeing someone's face isn't necessary for listening mindfully, it does help an incredible amount. Humans speak with their facial expressions just as much as they do with their voice. Be mindful of the small movements of their eyes, and the way lips form words. How often do they start to smile when they speak?

Of course, when practicing this exercise during a conversation with a living person, there's a danger of falling too deeply into meditation. A person might know that you are practicing mindfulness and will understand why you are so quiet and unresponsive, and why you concentrate so much on their face. But you can also find yourself in danger of weirding someone out. For other possible ways to listen mindfully, try the exercise with recordings. Podcasts have become an increasingly popular form of entertainment, and you have the privilege of listening to multiple sides of the conversation this way. A video podcast, too, will allow you to study faces alongside voices. Listening mindfully to multiple speakers is more difficult, but can prove more fruitful once you have mastered it. When training your ears to listen mindfully, however, it is better to stick with one speaker.

Apart from speaking, there is another way to listen mindfully, and that's through music. An unknown philosopher once postulated the question, "Has anyone ever actually listened to a song?" The statement, which almost seems like a joke at first, holds so much more weight when you sit down and think of the implications. How much do you actually listen to the music that you like? The multiple instruments or the overlaying of electronic tracks blend everything together in one sound. But have you truly listened to how each separate sound contributes to the whole? When do certain instruments kick in, and when do they fade out? The next time you have an opportunity to listen to your favorite song, don't just let it run through the familiar tracks. Listen to it as you've never heard it before. The variety of sounds, the meaning of the lyrics, the way the singer pronounces every word. One fantastic way to start picking up on a song's little individualities is by listening to a cover. Hearing two different interpretations of the same song makes it easier to identify how singers inflect words, and what instruments are being used where.

Using the method of listening mindfully in regards to a recording or a song can be practiced simultaneously with meditation. Playing music during meditation is sometimes recommended, but usually for music without lyrics so as not to get too distracted. When it comes to mindfulness meditation, however, it can be helpful to give the mind something to focus on, so using music with or without lyrics is equally helpful.

Flow Activities

A flow activity is anything that you do as a hobby. Usually, flow activities take the form of a sport or a creative outlet. Drawing, painting, writing, or sewing are the most popular of these. Cooking, too, is an effective activity. Hobbies, however, are not related to your work, and not something that we would do every day. Therefore, they are things that tend to be forgotten about or pushed to the side as we get older.

Pick out a flow activity for yourself. You can choose something that is already a hobby for you, or you can try out something completely new. When choosing, be aware that a flow activity is something you are physically doing with your body—so reading, unfortunately, does not count. Save reading for another time. Once you have chosen your flow activity, set aside a good chunk of time every week for it. Unlike meditation, which is recommended to start at ten-minute intervals, you will want at least an hour for your activity. If not more! Participating in activities like this requires time to warm up and really settle yourself into the motions of it, so a simple ten minutes just won't be enough. The time spent actually doing the activity has to be counted on top of warm-up time.

Now that you have chosen an activity and has time set aside, begin as you would normally. Don't bring mindfulness into it right away. This is the time you spend warming up, really getting into your groove. The reason flow activities are called such is because there's a flow to them, a rhythm to the movement. Sometimes this involves your whole body, like sports, but more often the movement is centered on your hands and arms. As you get into that movement get used to the flow, and make it to a point where your body is moving almost automatically. Now, you can begin to bring mindfulness into the equation.

Every mindfulness activity stimulates a different part of your mind. For listening and meditation, it is more about the observation. For flow activities, the lesson to be learned is more about the deliberation of each action. Say, for example, you were drawing. First, take into consideration how you hold your utensil. What are you drawing with? A pencil? Is it a wooden pencil, with a rounded tip of graphite, rolling more smoothly over the paper? Or is it a mechanical pencil? Does it leave a bit of resistance on the paper, the little stick of pencil lead almost creaking when you move it too slowly and press too hard? Or are you drawing with a pen, slower and more careful because you have no room for mistakes? Are you sketching with a crayon? Notice the way your fingers are bunched around it, but do this without looking. With your hand still moving, really take hold of the weight of the drawing utensil. Is it resting on your ring finger, your middle finger, or are you holding it evenly between all four? Do you hold it the way schools teach, or do you have your own special way unique to you and you alone? Are there calluses on your hand that indicate how often you've done this in the past or is it a relatively new experience?

Cast out your net of observation to the drawing itself. How does it look in the light? If you are drawing with a pencil, then certain places in it should shine in the lamplight. If you are using natural daylight, the overall coloration of the picture is going to look different. Plenty of artists nowadays like to draw on their computers, and rarely do it traditionally. Of course, there's no right or wrong way to make art, but for the sake of using mindfulness, you will need to put the computer or tablet away and make something with paper and a pen. The amount of detail you put into each piece of art is up to you. If you want to spend hours deep in mindful flow, line your art with a pen and color it with markers or pencil crayons. Don't stop until your mind says it's time.

This same outline goes for all flow activities. Painting is incredibly similar to drawing, with the slight difference of mixing paints together to get different colors. Coloring with markers or crayons does involve a bit of blending, but not to the same extent. When you are painting, you can be mindful of how each exact mix affects the shade of paint that you create. Paint also dries at a different rate than other materials, so be mindful of the way it dries. Forget that old adage that watching paint dry is boring. Be aware of how thicker mixtures dry slower, and how you avoid those areas and paint around other places. Be mindful of how painting over half-dry areas creates a different kind of color mixture. There are so many actions to be observed.

Most important to all flow activities is the deliberation of each movement. When you are sewing, deliberate on the color of the thread. When you are writing, consider carefully each word before you choose it. Typing won't deliver the same results—as with art, you will want to write the traditional way, with paper and pen. Shape each letter with careful precision. Mark the shape of it. These activities train your brain to always be deliberate in its actions, even when you are not purposefully in the same state of mindfulness. It doesn't happen right away, but with enough time, you will find yourself acting much more deliberately without meaning to. It becomes a kind of muscle memory.

Cooking is a nice difference because it doubles as a hobby and a necessity of life. You could cook your dinner every night, but you could also bake a batch of cookies for fun. So while cooking counts as a flow activity, it also can be adapted as a practice in your daily routine. More on that in our next chapter.

Observe Your Emotions

There's no real specific time or place best for observing your emotions, but a good recommendation is to go somewhere relatively unfamiliar. Whereas meditation is all about feeling comfortable, during this next practice, you want to have your mind somewhere it can be alert. Not on edge, as we don't want to cause unwanted stress but a place separate enough from your daily routine that you won't get lost in the comfort of familiarity. Going for a walk and finding a park bench on a route you don't usually travel is a perfect example.

What you are going to want to do in this practice is completely separate yourself from your emotions. Primary breathing exercises or other meditations can help you prepare for this. Or, rather than sitting on a public bench, you can keep walking. Taking in the scenery while thinking helps many stay calm, and it keeps another part of your mind practicing a different kind of mindfulness. It is two types of exercise at the same time.

Extricating yourself from your emotions is often far more difficult than anyone believes it will be at first. Primarily, this is because it involves admitting your own flaws and mistakes. It's not in human behavior to readily accept that we might have been wrong and see the error of our ways, but it is an important skill to learn, learning mindfulness or not.

There are two ways you can approach the exam. The first is to pick a specific event in which you were particularly emotional. As you look back on that situation, carefully catalog your emotions as though they didn't belong to you. Don't keep to baseline emotions, such as anger, or sadness. If a situation made you angry, examine what it was specifically that made you so angry. Was it a tight, hot frustration? Did you feel it more in your chest, or in your head? Did it cause a tightening in the lungs and a shortness of breath? Or is it a headache that wouldn't go away with a painkiller? Anger affects people in different ways. For some, it runs hot. Rage boils, its red, the negative subset of passion. For others, anger is a cold, almost clinical feeling. It can numb the fingers and freeze the words inside your mouth. When you are distanced from the emotion itself, you can see how you are affected by it in your own unique way.

Still thinking of the situation, consider what it was that made your emotions run so high. If you got angry, what were you angry at? Was it directed at a person, or was it the result of a situation that could not be avoided? Remember, the point of this exercise is to completely separate yourself from these emotions and examine them from an outside perspective, so if you feel that you are falling prey to the emotions; you need to take a step back and stop the examination. Do breathing exercise or meditate for a few minutes. Get yourself back into the headspace you were in before, where you and your emotions are two separate beings.

Examining your emotions is one of the hardest, but most helpful practices and the one that will affect you the most in the long run. It takes practice. That statement cannot be repeated enough—it takes practice, it won't happen right away, but eventually you will start to exhibit mindfulness without actively trying for it. Being able to separate yourself from your emotions helps when you find yourself in a highly volatile situation. Instead of losing control, your mind now knows how to take a step back and categorize what you are feeling as though it were happening to someone else. This means that not only are you in control of yourself, you also have the capability to take control of the situation. Once you have this kind of control, you can win most arguments, tackle a problem from the moral high ground, and even better understand the motivations of the people you argue with.

And though we've been using anger and arguments as an example, this isn't the limit to examining your emotions. Examine your sadness from an outside perspective as a way of dealing with grief. Examine your disgust, fear, or other opinions you may have that others condemn as irrational. Step away from it, can you see why others find you irrational? Is your fear rooted in something real, and if it is, can you start to find a way to move past it?

Easy enough, aren't they? Mindfulness, though it can be a tricky concept to grasp at first, it is so simple to put into practice. And it doesn't stop here—continue on to see how you can adapt it into your schedule.

Jon Goldstein
Chapter 5: Daily Lives of Mindfulness

Now that we have the basics of the practice under our belt, let's talk more about how we can implement mindfulness in our daily lives. Really, not all of us have the opportunity to sit for an hour and meditate every day. Some of us can't even afford to do that once a week. Between maintaining work or school, or both, a healthy social life, a good night's sleep, and the necessary time needed for relaxing the brain, it's just not feasible to carve away chunks of time each day to focus and center our minds.

Luckily, there are multiple ways to integrate mindfulness into your daily life. The following are a series of ways to healthily maintain a mindful state while going about your daily routine. As everyone's routine looks different, keep in mind that not all of these may apply to you. That's fine; again, this isn't a list of must-haves, it's an array of options. All anyone ever wants from mindfulness is to make themselves comfortable, so find little ways to make mindfulness fit you, personally.

Breathing Exercises

Go back to our first introduction to mindfulness: manual breathing. It's a very easy switch to flip in your mind. Now, pay attention to how you breathe. Thankfully, this is something you can do anytime, anyplace. Are you sitting at your computer doing work? Control your breathing while you type. Are you exercising? You're already in a position where you want to keep your breathing in fair control, so why not go the extra mile and put all your focus into it? This is the simplest of practices because anyone can do it, whenever they see fit. Do it now.

When You Walk

Do you go for a walk every day? If you don't, take that up immediately. Not just for the sake of mindfulness, but for every facet of your health. Even that little bit of exercise and fresh air stimulates your endorphins and will improve your overall mood. Of course, this book isn't a complete lifestyle guide, so let's get into how it pertains to mindfulness.

Walking is an unexpected sort of meditation. Generally, it is not considered part of the practice because it involves so much movement, but the meditation part comes from what you do with your mind while the rest of you move. While walking, take into account the deliberation put into each step. Think of how many different muscles go into each motion. Be mindful of each footfall. How does the sole of your foot feel? Are you walking on a sidewalk, concrete, or a gravel path? Can you feel the hardness of it through the soles of your shoes? Or are your shoes cushioned, giving a bounce with each step?

The lovely thing about walking mindfully is that you can sometimes double it up with other exercises, such as breathing or examining your emotions. Often times it works just as well to release pent-up emotions that have been building in you throughout the day. If you like to listen to music while you walk, pop the headphones in and listen mindfully. To a beginner, it is distracting to try both at once, so decide which you want to focus on. Music can just as easily become background noise as you walk, the more present part of your brain paying attention to the movement of your body.

Walking is much easier to fit into a daily schedule than a flow activity, or something that requires a significant amount of time carved out. You will also find it helps, regardless of whether you spend the entire walk being mindful.

All Five Senses

This is a small, easy practice that you can do anytime, anyplace, and without any kind of preparation. You can be doing absolutely anything, from lying in bed to working hard to kicking back and watching television. You can do it multiple times a day. Whenever you feel like it's time to try a little mindfulness on for size, go for the Five Senses.

The exercise is mostly what you expect, being called the Five Senses. What you want to do is take note and consider all five of your senses within a certain moment. Say, for example, you are at your place of work and have a quiet moment where you don't need to participate in a conversation.

- ❖ Start with sight. What are you seeing at that exact moment? What is the light source in the room, and how is it affecting your eyes? Do you find it strains a little, or is it darker than you'd like? Is the light natural, or coming from a fixture? If it is coming from both, see how they collide in certain places, and how shadows may fall into different directions. Then, observe all the objects within your view. Everything from furniture to other people in the room.
- ❖ Next, move on to your hearing. What does the room sound like at this particular moment? Is there any ambient music, perhaps a radio going? Is there the dull chatter of other people talking? Or are you

mostly surrounded by white noise? Can you hear any sounds from the outside world, perhaps through an open window? Focus, even, on the sound of your own breathing.

- ❖ After that comes the touch. What are all the sensory triggers? Start with your hands. Feel everything that they touch. Are you holding anything in your hand? When you move on up your arms, consider whether they are leaning on anything. Continue this process for every bit of your body. Feel how your legs are planted on the floor. Are you sitting on one, or both? Or does your job require you to stand? If it does, are you leaning on anything? Feel the weight of your clothes. Are they comfortable, or do you dress more for style? Consider everything, from the way the collar sits on your neck, to the way your shoes pinch at your toes. Are you a little sore? Do you need to stretch? Take a moment to do so, and be mindful of how everything feels when you stretch.

- ❖ Next, open your focus up to the smell of the room. While the previous three senses might be something you were already paying attention to, especially sight and sound, the smell is a sensation that tends to fade into the back of one's mind. Unless you are being presented with a very strong smell, your nose has most likely tuned everything down. Open it up again, and really take in the scents your workplace has to offer. Does it smell like paper and ink? Can you smell the dust off machines, or are they more likely to hold a whiff of cleaner and air freshener? Is anyone's perfume wafting about the space, perhaps yours? Are the general smells good, or do you notice that they aren't all that nice? If the latter, this may be a good time to invest in some relaxing scents for your workplace.

- ❖ Finally, focus on the fifth and final sense: taste. Save this one for last, if you can, because all too often, realizing that there is a specific taste in your mouth will send you off for a toothbrush or a mint or a stick of gum. Before you go running for the bathroom, be very mindful of the specific taste in your mouth. It may hold the hint of leftovers from your previous meal. It may still have some morning toothpaste's freshness. It may strike you as musty, and perhaps the only thing you can taste is dry. Drink some water for that, and consider how the liquid tastes on your tongue.

Some people feel open to a sixth sense, but choosing to focus on it as well could only prove to stress you out, the exact opposite of what you set out to achieve. You alone know the limits of what you feel in your possible sixth sense, so make that decision for yourself.

Body Scan

This is an exercise that began its life as a method for self-induced hypnosis. Fear not, for it has been repurposed multiple times. You won't accidentally find yourself wandering off in a trance. You may, however, find yourself falling asleep.

For optimal use, try the Body Scan when you go to bed at night. Consider it an alternative to counting sheep. It is mostly recommended to be done while lying down, and if you are already down and trying an exercise that calms you down, using it to help you sleep at night just seems like the logical thing to do. General anxiety and worry about the next day are what causes most people's inability to fall asleep at night. The other major factor is our bodies not calming down enough, usually due to a mixture of eating right before bed and looking at screens. Luckily, the Body Scan helps with both these problems.

When you lie down for bed, make sure your screens are put away. It's best to lie on your back, but you can certainly attempt it in any way that makes you feel comfortable. Once you are lying down, in the lighting that you prefer for sleeping, begin to scan your body from the bottom up.

Remember the scene from "Kill Bill," and the famous quote used, "Wiggle your big toe." You don't have to wiggle the toes for this exercise, but the main point is that you start small. Start with only one toe. Take a full catalog of it, every sensation that it feels. Is it warm? Is it a little chilly? Are you wearing socks, and does the fabric bush against it or cocoon it? Once you have fully taken account of this toe, move on to the next one, and repeat the process over again.

Move up from your toes to your feet. Scan one foot, then the other. Now try your ankles, and upwards. When you reach your torso, move out to your arms. Start again with an individual finger, and make sure each finger has been fully scanned and cataloged before you move on to one hand, and then the other. This exercise is called the Body Scan because you are treating your body as if it were moving through a very detailed scanner. Don't let any part of your body get missed or skipped over as you move up. It is also imperative that you don't move during this exercise. Tossing and turning is actually a cause of insomnia, not a symptom. If you gently force your body to stay still for a certain period of time, your brain registers it as slumber and thus, you fall asleep. If you can train your brain to feel happy, you can just as easily trick it to sleep.

High chances are, you will fall asleep before you reach your head, but in case you do, move into the previous Five Senses exercise as outlined before. Just do it to a lesser extent. Throughout all of this, be sure that you are feeling, as opposed to thinking. If you are actually running a monologue in your head, not only will you have trouble falling asleep, you will end up missing the point of the exercise entirely.

There is a very interesting addition you can give to most of these exercises, and that is to monitor the changes in your heart rate and breathing patterns. Although you may not always find yourself in a time where measuring your breath and your heartbeat for a few minutes is feasible, it is a very short measurement and isn't hard to stick in before and after. For one minute, count how many times your heart beats, and write it down. For the next minute, count how many times you breathe in, and breathe out. Perform the exercise, and once you have finished, count your heartbeat and breathing again for two minutes. See how much or how little it has changed. If your resting heart rate was already low, you won't really see much of a difference. But if you were feeling a little stressed or on edge beforehand, you can measure just how much mindfulness helps you. Seeing things on a physical scale can make them all the more real, and by measuring it out every day you can actually keep track of how much you are improving. Having proof that mindfulness is helping you like this helps motivate you to continue.

Chapter 6: The Fruits of No Labor

In the end, what are the benefits? Why even take up mindfulness in the first place? You've heard about how it can combat stress, addiction, or different disorders, but how exactly is it going to make your life better on the whole?

One of the first things to understand about the benefits of mindfulness is that you are getting rewarded for doing almost no work at all. Mindfulness is not something particularly difficult to work at, and while it does take time to fully change your mindset, it is not like pursuing a sport where you are constantly pushing your body to its limits. So far through this book, you may have gotten an idea of just how many varied benefits you receive while practicing mindfulness, but let's take a deeper dive into just how many fruits come from easy work.

Enhanced Immune System

Scientists have been fascinated with the effects mindfulness has on the human body, ever since the practice was first introduced to the Western world. To the surprise of everyone conducting the studies, mindfulness doesn't just have an effect on your emotions or your mental well-being. It actually has a positive impact on your physical immune system.

This baffles scientists because there seems to be no logical explanation as to why our ability to fight off colds and infections would be influenced by mindfulness. Is it a placebo? Possibly. Mindfulness is all about positive thinking, after all, and the belief that you are getting healthier can impact the way we perceive sickness. The placebo effect was coined after a study gave fake pills, filed with nothing but sugar, to patients with colds. The patients who had only taken sugar pills reported the same results as those who had taken real medication. And it seems that the same thing is happening with mindfulness. It's acting as a placebo, subtly influencing our expectations.

Fair enough, as it goes back to the Pollyanna Principle, and the research of Dr. Davidson. If you believe mindfulness is helping your immune system, then it is. Fake it until you make it.

But there are actually more layers at present as the interest in how mindfulness affected those afflicted with illnesses grew, so too did the study of how it affected certain groups of illnesses. Moving beyond the common cold, and past those suffering from PTSD, it has become a point of intense study and fascination among the medical community on how mindfulness has an effect on those with chronic or terminal illnesses.

This is not to say that mindfulness is a miracle healing system, and is the secret cure for cancer. Stop the search, we've figured it out! It's not going to "fix" anything. But there has been a remarkable amount of evidence gathered that mindfulness can lessen the severity of symptoms, and make illnesses easier to live with. Mindfulness relieves fatigue, and patients who practice mindfulness have a higher level of general energy than patients who don't. One of the marked studies, which aimed to outline the effects of mindfulness on cancer patients specifically, found that the patients who practiced mindfulness had a significant decrease in rumination and worry about the future.

It may be in part placebo, and it may be in part because mindfulness increases spirituality, and with that comes a feeling that your place in the universe is right and everything is happening as it is supposed to. But there is another, wilder explanation out there, one that many in the medical community don't want to explore. There is a mountain of historical records of spiritual healing, from all across the world. Any culture that practiced meditation, shamanism, trances, or anything related to the mystical 'third eye' would have an aspect of healing in their work. This did end up transmuting to other religions, most prominently in the faith healers of Christianity. But whereas most faith healers were proven to be frauds, the notion of spiritual healing has much more solid foundations. As mindfulness draws from many of these traditions, it stands to reason that spiritual healing may play a large part in the increased strength of the immune system.

Higher Brain Functioning

Have you ever found yourself trying to do work, but all you end up doing is staring at a blank page for hours on end, with absolutely no thoughts coming into your head? Everyone has been there. Sometimes our brains just refuse to function, and we draw a blank. Sometimes there's a genuine reason why your thought process is blocked, such as underlying stress factors. But sometimes, you blank out for absolutely no discernable reason.

It's a frustrating truth that everyone has to face, but the situations in which you find yourself blanking can vary in severity. You might get to the front of a drive-through, completely forget your order, and have to squint at the menu to remind yourself what you'd just been thinking about. Blanking on your personal information while filling out a form is a nuisance, but it's nothing that will affect you seriously. You can get up and find the information while muttering to yourself that, really, you should know this. But sometimes, blanking can cause you serious problems. Students commonly blank during tests, and the more important the test is, the more likely someone is to completely forget everything they know. All the hours spent studying can disappear right out the left ear. You could find yourself making an important presentation for work, and suddenly forget everything that you knew. Days, even weeks spent pulling this project together go down the drain, and no matter how much effort you put into it, you end up looking lazy.

Living mindfully means that your brain is less likely to blank out in any given situation. For one, you are working to eliminate the stress from your life. So those underlying factors that cause these brain shortages won't be a problem anymore. As for those mystery blanks, it also remains a mystery how mindfulness stops them from happening. The only thing you need to know is that they do.

The third hypothetical situation you find yourself blanking through is a confrontation or another moment where you need to think fast and on your feet. This one, in particular, is the most helped by mindfulness. We've mentioned before how mindfulness lets you separate from your emotions, controlling them in an argument and keeping your cool. But when you are living in the present moment, not only are you controlling your emotions, but your mind is calm and centered and able to deal with whatever is thrown at it. Instead of gaping silently because a certain comment or question has taken you off-guard, those who practice mindfulness are able to formulate proper responses quicker and tidier, meaning they won't be laced with emotions that you might regret later.

Having a higher brain functioning capacity doesn't mean you will be smarter, it means your mind will be more mature. That being said, those currently involved in academics will notice an improvement in their grades thanks to mindfulness. This is not a matter of being smarter, but of being able to manage your time, retain information, and use your mind to the best of its ability.

Bullying Defense

No matter where you go in life, you will have to deal with bullying on some form of the spectrum. Of course, it is highly prevalent in schools, from the earliest years of kindergarten, all the way through college years. But bullying doesn't end when you've graduated, although there's not nearly such a push or awareness of bullying in the workplace, which is perhaps why so many people tend not to realize that they're being bullied. But while mindfulness can't stop bullying, on the whole, it serves as a buffer to protect yourself, and could possibly help bullies change their behavior.

Let's start with schoolyard bullying. Like any other kind of behavioral problem, this can range. There are certainly kids out there with real undiagnosed disorders, who are not getting the help and support they need and therefore becoming a danger to others around them. But a very large portion of schoolyard bullies is only looking to get a rise out of their targets. It happens time and time again that the kids who don't really react to cruel words and taunts get left alone, while the ones who get emotional about it become repeat victims. Of course, it is never easy to shake off words that hurt you.

But by teaching children mindfulness, we can help them to keep a better control of their emotions and not react in such ways that will give the bullies what they want. Already, some schools have begun teaching children this kind of emotional control. Hopefully, it can also help bullies themselves by teaching them not to take out feelings of anger and frustration on other children. While, as with parenting, young children may have a hard time grasping mindfulness as a concept, you can certainly help them through certain exercises, in this case examining their emotions. As children often work better through a visual or kinetic medium, going through this exercise as an art project or playground game will help them understand. For example, remind them of the children's movie "Inside Out," and the way emotions were portrayed as unique figures with individual characteristics. If a child can visualize their emotions as these little people running around inside their head, they can 'pretend' to control them and therefore will gain better emotional control.

But children aren't the only ones who suffer from bullying. As stated beforehand, it is just as common to find bullying and harassment at your place of work. These problems are not always something you can take to head office, because unless something goes strictly against company policy, the head office will likely not do much to help you. Like the school system, everyday bullying goes ignored by figures of authority. Workplace bullying can manifest itself as someone pressuring you to take more shifts than you are capable of, or passive-aggressively inferring that if you don't complete a certain task you won't be able to keep your job. Young people especially find themselves the target of grunt work, being taken advantage of due to age, lack of experience, and a fear of complaining.

Mindfulness can keep you calm and centered on your own work. Having the strength to say that you cannot do certain tasks is taking responsibility, and should be heeded by your peers. You always want to work hard and do well but don't let yourself be taken advantage of. The emotional stability and decrease in stress that comes with mindfulness are marked with an increase in self-confidence. When you stand up for yourself in tandem with making your work better, respect for you will rise. Not only with the general workplace bullies back down, but there is a hope that your superiors will listen to you when you come to them with grievances.

Workplace Turnout

Continuing on from the last point, mindfulness will increase your productivity at work. Keep in mind what the staple of essentialism is. Don't get sucked into the thought process that productivity means a lot of work. If you are working fast, but the constant turnout is coming out at a lower quality than what you could do with time and care, your actual productivity isn't all that great and you will either be made to do things again, or be made out as a disappointing employee.

By infusing mindfulness and by extent essentialism into your work habits, the work that you do turn in will increase in quality and those kinds of things do not go unnoticed.

Erasing the Breakdowns

How many times have you suffered from a mental or emotional burnout? The answer is, likely more often than you think. People who work themselves too hard and don't take care of the mind or their emotions have become so accustomed to their way of life, that these 'off days' can start to feel like just a part of life. You find yourself emotionally frayed, crying at every little thing, unable to focus and crashing for periods of thirteen hours of sleep. It isn't healthy, and it isn't just a part of life.

What you've actually been experiencing is a burnout or a breakdown. You've taken on too much, and your body just shuts down. It's a little like your brain hitting the reset button. But your brain is a bit like a computer, and every I.T. person will assure you that holding the power button until the computer is forcibly shut down is not good for the technology.

A healthy body and mind do not suffer these burnouts so regularly. Honestly, a truly healthy body and mind don't suffer them at all, because they have dealt with the problems before they became too much to handle. Controlling your emotional state means that you won't become panicked or overwhelmed when a problem comes your way. Mindfulness creates this sense of stability, keeping you from overworking yourself, and regulating a proper sleep cycle. This internal stability staves off the body's need for a total shutdown. When you no longer suffer these regular burnouts, your overall quality of life improves considerably.

Brain Matters

Here's a fascinating bit of science that might gross you out – our brains have a certain level of malleability. It's not a muscle, no, it shouldn't change other than to grow and mature in tandem with our bodies. But actually, our brains can actually change their shape depending on a number of factors.

As our pioneer Dr. Davidson argued for the plasticity of the brain, it has been pointed out that certain changes in our body affect the cellular makeup of the brain. The 'grey matter' that brains are made of adapts due to events it has undergone. This is known in medical terms as 'neuroplasticity.' One of the most well-known examples of neuroplasticity is in patients who have suffered strokes. It has been found that grey matter can change shape or even shrink after a stroke, leading to a change in behavior and reduced capacity from those afflicted.

When applying mindfulness to the changing plasticity of the brain, it gives the opposite effect.

When practicing mindfulness and regular meditation, parts of your grey matter actually grow in mass. Most prominently we see this in the cerebral cortex and the left hippocampus. Your cortex is the part of your brain meant for attention, sensory perception, thought, and consciousness. Looking at all these terms, you can see it reflected back the things you exercised in mindfulness. The left hippocampus, on the other hand, is in charge of your memory. If are wondering how mindfulness can lead to an ability to retain more information, here's exact proof of how. On top of these two, mindfulness can also reduce the amygdala—the part of your brain that triggers a fight or flight response. This is one proven way that mindfulness reduces stress and anxiety.

The fascinating thing about the neuroplasticity of the brain is that it provides the one solid, physical piece of evidence that mindfulness is more than just a therapeutic exercise, and it does more for your body in the long term than just change your outlook. It provides an argument to naysayers that they'll have a hard time disputing, and it is something that you can hold on to as you begin down the path of mindfulness, an assurance that this isn't all for nothing.

In the end, it all boils down to the same conclusion; an overall improvement in your quality of life. Because that's what mindfulness is really all about; the big picture, as opposed to the little details. Every day that you live mindfully is better than a day you don't.

But all this sounds maybe too good to be true. Let's be pragmatic. You want to know if there's a risk to mindfulness. So let's delve into this topic head-on.

Jon Goldstein
Chapter 7: No Risk, No Reward

Are there really any risks to starting the practice of mindfulness? It's an easy answer to say no, but there's more to the issue than what appears at first. Every kind of spiritual endeavor brings a level of risk to the table, even something as simple and clean as mindfulness. Before you get scared, know that these risks are not guarantees of bad things that will happen! On the contrary, your hope is that nothing bad will come of mindfulness. But why do we study history? To learn from humanity's past mistakes and try not to follow down those same dark paths. It's the same principle here. Know the risks before going in, so you can avoid them altogether.

Getting Lost

The basic and broadest risk that you face when setting your mind is the risk of pulling away too far. Cutting out the unimportant things in your life can become addicting, and if you aren't careful, you'll find yourself cutting out the important things, too.

While mindfulness springs from Buddhist traditions, the last thing you want to do is find yourself turning into a monk. Spending so much time inside your head doesn't mean you can't exist outside of it. Living outside your head is healthy, and your practice in mindfulness should strengthen the relationships you have with friends and family, not let them wither on the vine. Solitude is good and necessary for some meditation, but don't let yourself get lost in it.

Getting Lazy

One flaw that's a little more centered on certain types of people is the habit of getting lazy. Take essentialism, for example. The noble pursuit of quality over quantity is easily swayed in the direction of laziness. Instead of doing less in order to do a better job, you find yourself doing less because you just want to slack. Essentialism allows procrastinators and slackers a rationale for their behavior, and it makes it easy for someone like that to say that they're only doing one thing a day because essentialism tells them to. High chances are, they're barely doing that one task. Complacency and sloth are two flaws that go hand in hand, and before you know it, you could find yourself resting all day—quite the opposite of the essentialist principles you started out with.

If you know you are a procrastinator, be very aware of this before taking up essentialism. It's hard to set up a goal chart, but if you have a day planner or calendar, just mark in it the thing you plan to devote yourself to that day. That way, you can look back on the week and reflect on whether you did those things to the best of your ability. If you find that essentialism just isn't having an effect on your work quality that you wanted, take it out of your mindfulness approach. It's only a subset, after all, and not necessary to fulfilling mindfulness. Being aware of your own flaws and shortcomings, and finding ways to work around them, is part of being enlightened.

Increased Anxiety

This one seems like it's all backward. Mindfulness is supposed to reduce anxiety, not increase it. But it has been reported from several accounts that their attempts to practice mindfulness actually led to an increase in their stress and worry, which was completely unexpected and they were quite unprepared for. These cases sprang from people who did not fully grasp the concept of mindfulness before starting, and thus it was practiced wrong from the start.

One explanation for why practitioners could find increased stress levels could be due to not meeting expectations as quickly as you thought. Do not go into mindfulness with the idea that your moods will drastically increase or change immediately. Someone may practice mindfulness for a week and, when they find it has not decreased stress levels as they thought it would, that stress may pick up. There are two flaws with this kind of mindset. Firstly, don't expect mindfulness to make a huge impact on your thought process immediately. Learning to practice mindfulness is a slow process. Secondly, the practitioner seems to believe that mindfulness is like a kind of 12-step program. Do it for a certain amount of time, your anxiety will go away, and you can go back to the way your brain worked before!

Mindfulness is not a 12-step program. It is a full lifestyle change. There is no end goal, no stopping point. Complete immersion is what mindfulness aims for, becoming so adept at the practice that it becomes ingrained in your subconscious mind and this is a daily part of your routine. The idea is that you will no longer have to think about it because mindfulness will just be something you do. And anyone who has ever tried to permanently change their routine can vouch that it doesn't happen overnight.

So, don't let the worry that it isn't working right away take over. It's impossible to ignore the voices in your head, telling you that you're doing it wrong, but work against them. Keep to the outlines suggested in this book, and it will become second nature. All you need is patience and dedication.

Rumination

It's important to bring this up because rumination is the opposite of mindfulness, and yet the two are so easy to confuse for one another that you may find yourself mired in rumination rather than mindfulness. This is one of the key mistakes people make, leading to the aforementioned increase in anxiety.

Rumination, a psychological issue, is a hyper-focusing on your own symptoms of distress. It means that you are so fixated on the cause of your stress and worry that you cannot actually begin the process of clearing your head. Because both rumination and mindfulness involve a deep thought process about the goings on inside your own head, it is very easy for a person already suffering anxiety to confuse one for the other.

Mostly, rumination involves overthinking our own failures. Combat against this feeling by admitting to yourself that it is okay to make mistakes. If you are failing to meet your goals, take a step back and decide if the goals you set for yourself were too much. Starting small is a good way to begin progress because you can easier accomplish smaller tasks, and the positive reinforcement your brain gives you then feeds into the energy you need to reach larger goals.

Chapter 8: Answering Your Questions

It's safe to assume that, by now, you have a lot of questions about mindfulness that haven't been covered by the previous chapters. Or, maybe you saw the title to this chapter and skipped right ahead. Here are the most frequently asked questions about mindfulness, and their answers.

Q: If the meditation and mindfulness practices are easy one day, but difficult the next, am I doing it wrong?

A: Actually, that's an indicator that you're doing it just right. By being able to tell that some days come easier than others, you are already observing how mindfulness affects you and the way you perceive the world. Keep at it, and make a note of why certain days are harder. Likely, a pattern will begin to emerge. Perhaps you start every week calmly, centered, and mindful, but as the weekend approach you to start losing your grip. Perhaps looming deadlines cause your grip on the reins to slip. It can even come down to something as simple as certain personal interactions you have. Once you notice a pattern, you can work on adapting your mindfulness exercises around it. If you notice that a certain upcoming day has one of your 'triggers', do what you can to get in more exercise, or do some extra meditation in the morning.

Q: I can't be mindful as soon as I begin to participate in a conversation. Is that ever going to get better?

A: Short answer, yes. While listening mindfully is one of the first practices you try, its weakness is given away in the title: listening. Getting yourself dragged into the flow of the conversation means you can easily lose a grip on your mindfulness. What you want to do is take it slowly and methodically. If you're in a conversation where listening mindfully is too difficult, don't try. Striving for mindfulness undercuts the purpose of mindfulness itself, and if you are too focused on keeping mindful, you won't be really present and your conversational partner is going to get fed up. Find topics where someone is going to be talking to you for long periods of time, with little participation required from you, and use that time to listen mindfully. Continue to do it on your own time, listening to recordings or music. Talk aloud to yourself, and try listening mindfully to your own voice. As you grow more adept at mindfulness as a whole, participating in conversations while staying mindful will come naturally to you.

Q: Is mindfulness damaging? Is it going to unblock any great emotional traumas?

A: Absolutely not. We've outlined the risks of mindfulness already, and though they do exist, there's nothing that could be classified as damaging. Moreover, with the right knowledge and preparation going into it, you will be able to avoid any of these risks. As for unblocking emotional trauma, this is the opposite of what mindfulness does for you. Mindfulness is used by therapists for clients suffering from post-traumatic stress disorder, something that they certainly wouldn't do if it could potentially make things worse in any way.

There's no clear source for some of the malicious rumors spread about mindfulness, indicating that it is dangerous or damaging. The only possible way to get that end result is to miss the point of mindfulness completely, and instead of separating yourself from your emotions, you repress them. Everything within this book teaches you mindfulness properly, so you are in no danger of accidentally repressing your emotions. It's about controlling them, not pretending they don't exist.

Q: How long do I have to wait before seeing results?

A: We've touched on this several times, as this question differs from a person to person basis. The general answer is, "A while." Mindfulness takes time, it takes practice, and there is no real point that you can reach to say, there—I am now successfully a mindful person. The benefits of it will kick in slowly and often so subtly that you won't really notice them until they're well underway. Patience is one of the keys to mindfulness as a whole, and a watched pot will never boil. Sitting and waiting for results to happen will only hinder your progress. It helps to not think of it as 'results'. Instead, think of this as a long-term lifestyle overhaul.

Q: If sitting still is so important to meditation, how does a person with ADHD practice it?

A: Some people with ADHD take up mindfulness for the express purpose of learning to sit still. One of the most unique benefits to mindfulness is that it helps with restless leg syndrome. But if sitting still is something out of the question for you, don't let that stop you. Instead, incorporate movement into your practices. So many mindfulness exercises involve being aware of all five senses, and adding the awareness of your own movement is certainly doable. You can also bring yoga stretches into your meditation.

Instead of sitting or lying still, do some poses. If even that proves too difficult, take up walking and meditate while you walk. It is harder, but not out of the realm of possibility. It's easier than attempting to sit still, and being overwhelmed with frustration when you can't manage it. Even just walking back and forth, up and down a hallway is enough. Focus your energy on flow activities, and build your mindfulness from there. You should certainly never be made to feel excluded, or that you cannot participate in meditation just because you have ADHD.

Q: Continuing on, so many of these exercises involve using all five senses. How does someone with a physical disability participate?

A: Great question. Always be mindful of how someone's disability might impair their ability to practice meditation and mindfulness. As with ADHD, find ways to work around it. So you have a visual impairment. You remove 'sight' from the five sense equation. Same goes for hard of hearing people. If you already aren't relying on this sense, then there's no reason to feel bad or improper for leaving it out of sense awareness. If your disability is more about mobility, then move the focus of your energy to exercises that don't involve movement. There is a good chance that you will be more adept at meditation, to begin with. In this case, you have the advantage. You are just as right as anyone else for mindfulness, and don't let anything you hear convince you otherwise!

Jon Goldstein
Chapter 9: A Little More About a Little Less

While we talked about essentialism and minimalism back in chapter three, we didn't really go into specifics on how to really put those into practice. Here, we're going to go a little more deeply into how you can do a little less.

Declutter Your Life

Firstly, take a look at how much excess surrounds you. If you went cleaning a room as part of mindfulness exercising, you might get an idea of just how much we surround ourselves with unnecessary objects. Are these things really helping us? Is it making you feel better to have junk all around you? Probably not.

Even if you think you are the kind of person who enjoys clutter, it has an effect on our subconscious. When you cast your gaze out to any given point in a room, every object that you see has a load of information being sent to your brain. Not only are your eyes taking into account every little object, but your memory is assigning little bits and pieces to each one. This kind of information overload is what causes us to see the world so shallowly, and prevents us from a true appreciation of any one single thing. Clutter is fine in some places only if it makes you comfortable, but give yourself spaces where you are simple and open. At work and at home, bring the minimalist principles into your decor and make your spaces as clean as they can be.

Some Similar Concepts

Essentialism and minimalism, despite being under-umbrella terms themselves, have a number of even more focused and similar ideologies that you can adapt while practicing mindfulness. Learning about these will help you further shape mindfulness into the unique process that works best for you.

Wakefulness

You're in this state of consciousness every day, its part of your brain function. All you need to do is be awake. So how does this relate to mindfulness at all? Well, the longer you are awake, the more your cerebral cortex works. And your cerebral cortex is one of those bits of the brain most affected by mindfulness. Burnouts, naps, and long periods of sleep decrease the power of the cortex, so mindfulness works in tandem to bring your brain to the height of its ability. Maintaining a state of wakefulness boosts your mindfulness, and in turn, mindfulness keeps you in a longer, healthier state of wakefulness. It's a mutually beneficial system.

Prudence

Is this a lovely girls' name used by the Puritans because it is classically considered to be one of the Seven Heavenly Virtues? Yes. Is it a state of mind which we can keep ourselves to better our lifestyle in concordance to mindfulness? Also yes.

Prudence, meaning 'to see ahead', or 'foresight', has often been conflated with caution. Though these words have similar definitions, they aren't one and the same and have led to the concept of prudence as being seen as old-world, stuffy, and negative. Prudence, or Prudentia, the name of a goddess in Roman times, is the personification of foresight and wisdom. It is not the reluctance to take risks. It is simply the knowledge of when to step back when the risk is too great. A much more accurate description of prudence would be 'practical wisdom.'

The difference between knowledge and wisdom, also commonly conflated with one another, is usually defined thusly: Knowledge is knowing a tomato is a fruit, but wisdom is knowing not to put a tomato in a fruit salad. A prudent person might consider putting a tomato in a fruit salad but decides that it will ruin the overall flavor and presentation, and it would better serve on a cracker with cheese.

Prudence involves weighing the circumstances before acting and making the proper decision of whether the risk is worth taking. It involves making sound judgment calls, and eventually being able to rely on your own instinct. If you gain a reputation for yourself as a truly prudent person, you will find yourself the one people come to for advice, or to make the hard decision that nobody else wants to tackle.

As you practice mindfulness, your ability to make decisions will improve. By bringing a sense of prudence into your thought process and using it in tandem with a sense of mindful detachment, you will reach the peak ability for rational judgment.

Conscientiousness

This is considered one of the staples of the human personality, and it walks the same road as prudence. Being a part of the HEXACO personality model means that much more study and observation has gone into conscientiousness and how it affects the people who live with it.

Conscientiousness is the facet of mindfulness in deliberation, and the ability to think carefully before you act. Remember, in mindfulness, every action you take is done with great deliberation and nothing is wasted. So, too, you use conscientiousness to make sure you never waste a moment. By using conscientiousness, you guarantee that you are living in the present and every moment is being used to the fullest, just as mindfulness should be.

You can bring conscientiousness into your life by keeping your workspace clean and without distraction. Organize what you do have. For example, the books you have on a bookshelf can be put in alphabetical order, or color-coded, or even categorized by genre. Keep daily planners and make yourself to-do lists. Check things off as you do them each day.

A low level of conscientiousness is directly related to your levels of laziness and procrastination, so increasing its presence in your daily life is not only beneficial to your mindfulness, it is beneficial to how you live your life on the whole. If you are looking to bring essentialism into your work life but know that you run the risk of getting lazy, work on your levels of conscientiousness. Bring them up to keep yourself focused, on task, and completing the things you set out to do every day.

On the flip side, if your levels of conscientiousness are too high, you run the risk of overworking yourself and becoming too obsessed with your work. Don't let this happen, and remember to keep to the essentials. In your daily planner, outline exactly what you want to accomplish that day. Do no less, but do no more. Once you have done what you planned to the very best of your ability, close the planner, close the folders, and turn to relaxation. It's all about keeping the balance.

Observation

This is the facet of mindfulness that reminds us; observe the world as it is happening as an impartial viewer. The origin of observation comes from philosophy, by taking the input of information, observing, and categorizing it rationally, as opposed to emotionally. You automatically partake in observation while involved in mindfulness meditation. Once you have observed the information, you can absorb it, and make a rational and informed decision.

Most of the previous ideologies involve some form of decision-making and rational thought. That's a part of mindfulness that doesn't really get touched on as often because for many, 'mindful' and 'rational' aren't really in the same sphere of thinking. But they have far more similarities than you realize at first. This rationale is not only going to make your life better, but it will help you become the best version of yourself.

Alertness

Alertness is the state of being completely aware and ready for reactions. A subset of mindfulness, alertness is one of the most vital things our body needs, while simultaneously being the one it never has.

It seems to be in human nature to struggle with alertness. We are constantly pumping our systems full of drugs and caffeine to achieve the desired state of alertness. Not only in this unhealthy, but it also isn't giving the truly desired reaction you need. These methods of staying alert come hand in hand with shaking hands, poor decision-making, an increased heart rate, and can result in a state of hyper-awareness where you aren't any more productive than you would be asleep. So why is it that we struggle with alertness? Isn't this something that should come naturally?

Yes, it is, but our lives have become so unnatural and ever-changing that the human body has not evolved or adapted to it. We never get the proper amount of sleep that we need, nor do we ever properly distribute time between work and relaxation. Some are all work and no play, exhausting the mind and causing the aforementioned reliance on caffeine to get through the day. But the opposite problem of all play and no work has equally disastrous results. Sleeping for too many hours a day causes the brain to tire, and you end up sleeping even more. Becoming too dependent on relaxation and downtime leads to a weak spirit, and when the time comes that you really need to buck up and work, you can't because you have no energy left at all. Once again, you fall on caffeine to get you by.

If you are a young person, likely a college student, question whether you have uttered the joking phrase, "Don't talk to me before I've had my coffee." Chances are, you and everyone around you have said it at least once. Even though it is a joke, don't overlook what the statement implies and that is you have an addiction. You now rely on caffeine to achieve the state of alertness that humans are supposed to be able to achieve naturally and really should be experienced throughout the entire day.

Mindfulness can help relieve you from this need for coffee. It will help even out your sleep cycle. Essentialism can help you create the much-needed balance between work and play, preventing you from getting too bogged down and overworked, but keeping you motivated enough to do work every day and not become so lazy that you can't do any work at all. Though, this doesn't mean that you have to stop drinking coffee. It tastes good, after all. But you won't find yourself on the verge of death without it.

Chapter 10: Mindfulness-Based Stress Reduction

Don't be surprised that the scientifically proven method of Mindfulness-Based Stress Reduction, or MBSR, was only mentioned once in the course of this book. Here is everything you need to know about MBSR. If you want mindfulness to specifically hone in on dealing with your stress or anxiety, this is the way to do it.

It has its home as a program at MIT, founded by Jon Kabat-Zinn in 1979. The three tenements of the program that he sets in place are meditation, body awareness, and yoga. But you don't have to travel to MIT to participate in the program itself, as the lessons are open for anyone on the Internet, and some of the guided meditation that Kabat-Zinn led is available in audio format on YouTube.

Upon reaching the Center for Mindfulness website, you are entreated to the following before you embark on the program. Turn the following into a challenge, instead of a chore. Make it something you strive for, because it rewards you, not something you're forced to do because you're supposed to. You have to want it.

The time set out for practitioners is 45 minutes a day, 6 days a week. You will notice right away that this is a far cry from the recommended 10 minutes a day meditation begins at. This is because MBSR is a specific program. Going into it, you are not so much aiming for a slow lifestyle change. It is more like a training camp, a dedicated regimen. When actually involved in the program, you would be going into the clinic for this time every day, alongside a mass of other people taking the course. If you are trying to emulate MBSR without attending the classes, as if you've purchased this book that was likely your plan, keep to this same attendance. Outline a certain 45 minutes out of every day that you dedicate, and keep them the same time every day, as if you were part of a class.

The Raisin

The first exercise anyone is taken through in MBSR is the well-known Raisin Exercise. While any kind of food can realistically be used, the raisin is recommended because it is small enough that it won't overwhelm the senses, and it has an interesting and unique enough texture that will stimulate the mind.

The first thing to do upon taking the raisin is to pretend that they have never seen a raisin before. While you can't exactly erase the memory of knowing a certain thing exists, you can steer your thoughts in that direction. Cast your mind back, if you can, to the very first time you saw or ate a raisin. Relive that sensation.

Now that you are looking at a raisin with new eyes, take in the entire sight of it. Exploring the visuals of a thing is a key component to mindfulness. Think of the way you normally look at food before you eat it. You are looking, but are you really seeing? Observe all the ridges on the fruit, the exact coloration of the skin, and how the light hits it. Is the raisin slightly translucent, golden brown, a bit like an amber stone, with the light shining through? Or is it dark, the color solid and impenetrable?

As you fully appreciate the look of the raisin, turn your mind to how it feels. Is it slightly squishy? Does it give between your fingers? Or is it hard and little crusted at the edges? If you rolled it around in your fingers, what would give more? Is it the raisin or the pads of your fingers?

Now that you've got a solid grasp on the look and feel of the raisin, put it in your mouth. Continue to mind the feel of it, but now instead of using your hands, you are feeling with your teeth and tongue. Alongside this comes the burst of flavor. Be mindful of that as well, taking into account exactly where and how you feel it on your tongue.

All in all, by the time you've swallowed, it should have taken up about five minutes. While this is a practice you can do on your own, the guided audio for it is available on the Internet. You can listen to Kabat-Zinn himself guide you through, as though you were really participating in the MBSR program itself.

Even though this is only the introduction to the MBSR program, the Raisin Exercise can prove extremely useful as a starting point to calm you down from a stressful situation. Keep a bag of raisins or other fruits or nuts that you enjoy, on your person, it means that at any given time you can take a step back and go through these motions once again. Not only can this serve as a reset point to help you calm down from whatever stressful situation you have found yourself in, having a healthy snack is always beneficial.

Examine Your Stress

In an earlier chapter, we talked about one of the strongest and most vital practices of mindfulness which is examining your emotions. We went over how emotions like anger, sadness, and fear, can be separated and looked at objectively. The goal of the practice is to let these negative emotions go and find the root of what causes them in the first place. Learn to separate ourselves from our emotions in times when they run high, therefore not letting ourselves be dictated by these emotions at the moment and taking control of the situation. But nowhere in life does this come in as useful as much as it does when it pertains to stress.

Separating yourself from stress is the hardest emotion to tackle, and the one that takes the most practice and experience. Anyone who has experienced anxiety in any form knows just how it feels—like a sticky, black sludge. It pulls you down and doesn't want to let go. Total separation might have to come with some visualization exercises. See yourself as scraping away the sludge with tools, like an archaeologist chipping centuries of dirt away from the beautiful artifact beneath.

Stress is not hard to find the root of. It usually manifests as a direct result of a situation, or a general unease about the world at large, and these two usually overlap. So, in the process of separating and examining stress, don't spend so much time looking to where it came from. Instead, focus the energy on leaving it behind. Once you have successfully been able to separate yourself from the other emotions, you should be experienced enough to try it with your stress.

Therefore, when you feel the panic begin clawing its way up your throat, step away and begin to separate from it. This practice is the most useful when it comes to the situations themselves. If you need to step away and go somewhere quiet to calm down, then do so and never feel ashamed about having to ask. As you grow more and more adept, however, you will find yourself able to separate your emotions automatically. Though anxiety is a heavy beast of burden to tackle, at least by opening yourself to examining it, you can stop it from overwhelming you.

Focus vs. Awareness

Within the MBSR program, there are two kinds of mindfulness outlined; focused mindfulness and awareness mindfulness. The difference between these two can be easily understood by going back to our two postulated meaning of mindfulness. Focused mindfulness is being mindful of something, while awareness mindfulness is having your mind be full of things. Are those the proper dictionary definitions? No, probably not, but it's a simple and easy way to connect them with everything we've learned so far.

While practicing focused mindfulness, you want to focus your attention on a certain single thing, and take it all in. The Raisin Exercise, as outlined above, is a perfect example of this. The object of focused mindfulness is to see the complete value of everything, how each individual piece of the universe is special in its own way. This leads to our deliberation, consideration, and the realization of our own place in the world.

Awareness mindfulness, on the other hand, is more about seeing the forest for the trees. It's absorbing everything, all at once. This is what we use when we examine our emotions. Rather than being rooted in the present, awareness mindfulness allows us to float a little, to navigate the space inside our own heads. It also takes the interesting approach of viewing yourself and your life from an outside perspective. Don't think of it as someone else studying you, because that will lead to an instinctive worry that this outside perspective is judging you. That's just you, subconsciously judging yourself. Try instead to look at it from a non-human, otherworldly perspective.

Both kinds of mindfulness are linked to one another, and you cannot truly achieve a state of mindfulness if you are practicing one but not the other. For the MBSR program, however, you are encouraged to try and shift between one and the other. Begin in a state of focused mindfulness, by trying either the Raisin Exercise or something else. Once you've come to a state of being completely focused and in the present, move to a state of awareness mindfulness. Expand your perspective from one small thing, to everything around you.

And it doesn't have to stop with switching from one to the other. As you grow more comfortable with this switching, you can go back to being focused again. If you find it helpful for you, go back from one to the other multiple times. Being able to discern the difference between these two kinds of mindfulness leads you to understand what will help you in any given situation. Is this a moment where you need to be present and focused? Or is your crisis internal and you needed to step away from it? By practicing the shift between the two, not only will you be able to discern which will help you, but you can also call upon the specific state of mind you need at that moment. You have been training yourself to become either focused or aware on command.

Object Meditation

This is another simple and helpful way to practice focused mindfulness. Though very similar to the Raisin Exercise, object meditation does not require you to make use of your full five senses.

Much like the Body Scan, the practice of object meditation has been around for far longer than mindfulness itself. It was co-opted by mindfulness practitioners, who saw just how useful it was to serve their purposes. Object meditation was never about putting yourself into a trance, however. Instead, it is a quick way to center yourself in the present at any time.

- ❖ First, pick an object to focus on. It works best when the object you pick is nothing too fancy. Size matters, in this case. If your object of choice is too small, there won't be enough for you to focus on to reach a state of real meditation. But for the purposes of MBSR, you'll likely want to carry this object around with you, so it can't be anything large or bulky.
- ❖ The object can have different significance to you, depending on the kind of person you are, and your belief system. A small statue or figure of a religious icon work for many people. If you are someone who draws a lot of power from sentiment and

nostalgia, special jewelry or a childhood toy will have the most effect. In the end, you know best what kind of object to focus on. If you want something that you know you'll have on your person at all times, try a cell phone.

- Now that you have your object, focus on it. Shave away all outside sensations. Put yourself in a moment where nothing else in the world exists, save for you and this object.
- In order to begin meditation, close your eyes and count backward. The number is up to you, but the best numbers to count down from are five, seven, and ten. When you have counted down to zero, open your eyes. You have begun meditation.
- While meditating on this object, take into account everything about it. All details, from the way it looks, to the way it feels if you are holding it. This is why very small objects cause problems. For one, you can strain the eye trying to study the details.

For two, you quickly run out of things to notice.

- ❖ Keep at the meditation. Anytime you feel your mind straying, attempting to focus on something else, bring it back into the present. Keep all your attention on the object only.
- ❖ The real trick is to observe only. If you start running a narrative in your head, labeling pieces of the object, you aren't doing it properly. Close your eyes, count backward, and start again.

In general, object meditation exists as a way to help us notice the details in everything. In our daily lives, we have so much information coming from us from so many different places, that our minds cannot truly focus on one thing fully. Most of the information we get is absorbed only at a surface level, not enough for us to truly appreciate it. Object meditation teaches us to observe things more carefully and to take things in at more than just surface value.

But as to why object meditation is so helpful for stress reduction, in particular, it's once again very similar to the Raisin Exercise. It serves as a reset for your mind when stress threatens to overwhelm you. And this is why you want your object to be something you can carry with you every day. Whenever you feel like you need to calm down, you can take a moment to yourself, and begin meditation. It doesn't have to be a long time—you could do it for five minutes and it would still prove helpful.

Worry Surfing

Don't confuse this for examining your stress. Similar as they are as an idea, there's a different set of rules to play by when you attempt the Worry Surf. Opening yourself up to the examination of your anxiety is good in theory, but not always possible in practice. This exercise in clear visualization is all about dealing with a panic attack as it comes.

The symptoms of an oncoming panic attack pinpoint around four general signs:

1) Heart palpitations.

Your heartbeat starts to kick up at an immense pace, and it happens very quickly, causing shortness of breath and often dizziness.

2) Sweating.

Yes, an excess of sweating happens for a lot of reasons, including embarrassment. But sweating is also an indicator of an oncoming panic attack, and usually is the first one you can spot. A sudden wave of heat and prickling at your skin can warn you that a panic attack is on the way.

3) Shaking.

Your entire body starts to tremble, often to the point where you cannot walk properly, or hold anything in your hands.

4) Chest pains.

If you were already having trouble breathing because of how fast your heart has begun to beat, you can imagine how much harder it becomes when your lungs start to feel like they've shrunk. A person undergoing a panic attack is usually incapable of taking a deep breath, due to this feeling.

Panic attacks are more common than people realize, and are not always part of diagnosed anxiety. While that may mean that you experience them more often, and have even found ways of working through it on your own, people who rarely experience panic attacks won't know it's coming. Some don't realize what's happening to them, and others downplay it because they aren't ready to come to terms with the fact that they have suffered a panic attack.

Don't ever let the stigma affect you. There's nothing wrong with admitting to having a panic attack. It's far more dangerous to not admit that you need help and to never find ways to adapt and work through it. Instead, when you feel the oncoming symptoms, try this exercise.

The Worry Surf is visualization, meaning you have to see things like a picture inside your mind. Get as poetic and metaphorical with it as you want—it's all inside your own head, nobody's going to laugh or judge you.

When you feel these symptoms coming, visualize them as a great wave. With the intensity that comes with these emotions, the wave is likely dark water, brown or blackish, white-capped and cresting. It's coming to drown you, to pull you under. But you aren't going to let it. Don't try to stop the wave from coming. Trying to stop panic attacks by forcing them down never works and usually makes them worse off than they were already. Instead of fighting it, continue to see the wave build higher and higher as it comes toward you. Let the wave get as tall as it can, and then, right before it crashes over you, visualize yourself surfing over it.

It's like one big, long breathing exercise. You breathe in continuously and repeatedly until you feel the pressure and your lungs are about to burst, and then you let it all back out again. Instead of succumbing to panic or trying to fight it, you take the third option of going over it. Depending on how big the wave is, visualize yourself riding it out for miles, all the way until you no longer feel in danger of panicking. To fully immerse yourself in this picture, add little details. Things like the wind ruffling your hair, the smell of salt water, the sun shining on your skin. Go the full distance and put together a mental surfboard, with unique colors and a decal that you like. Imagine the feel of it beneath your bare feet.

The Worry Surf is not guaranteed to work right away, but as you practice other facets of mindfulness, it becomes easier and more natural. Once you learn how to do it, the impact it will have on your life is phenomenal. Many people assume that, because they can't find a way to stop having panic attacks, that there's no hope. You can't stop a panic attack from coming, but you can ride out that wave. Don't let it drown you.

Yoga

What makes yoga truly so helpful for MBSR is that you can find audio of Jon Kabat-Zinn guiding you through it anywhere on the Web.

Yoga has long been used as a way to practice meditation, and so too does it get used for mindfulness. While not specifically something the fight off stress, yoga is a prominent piece of the MBSR program because it puts your body in the same good place as your mind. Take a yoga mat anywhere you want to practice. Indoors, outdoors, on your own or with people, it doesn't matter. Set up your sound system—play through a computer, a phone, headphones, whatever works for you. Let the masters take you through this one. Yoga can be done on your own, but when guided you'll know you're always making optimal use of your body.

The Seven Foundational Attitudes

At a closer look, Jon Kabat-Zinn has outlined seven attitudes that come with mindfulness. These are the attitudes that you are striving towards. Mindfulness itself does not have an end goal, but the MBSR program does because it is a course that finishes over a set amount of weeks. When you have reached these seven attitudes, you will know that you've succeeded.

1. Non-Judging

This doesn't just mean not judging others. It means not judging the world as a whole, and most importantly, not judging yourself. By using mindfulness, you become an impartial observer to the world around you. Bring in the element of observation into your life, and pay attention to the way your brain may make a snap judgment of someone or something based on observation alone. A mindful person will not make these judgments, as they base opinions only on the information that actually becomes absorbed into the mind.

2. Patience

A mindful person has the patience for all things; people, the cars on the highway, and the flow of time itself. Believe that things are happening at a certain pace for a reason. The stream of the universe isn't unbalanced; all you need to do is sit back and let it happen. This patience leads to a contentment and is the main reason why your stress and worry about the future dissipates. Hold in your heart the belief that you are on the path you're meant to be on, and things will work out the way they were always meant to, in due time. Bring that patience with you in your interactions with others. Human relationships grow most from positive feedback. If you exhibit patience and kindness to an individual, they will return it to you, again reducing another factor of stress in your life.

3. Beginner's Mind

Even someone who has mastered mindfulness keeps a beginner's mind. Always be open to new paths; never be afraid to try something new. You may be experienced at one thing, but that shouldn't stop you from trying it another way. Remember prudence and conscientiousness. It isn't that you shouldn't take risks. Rather, weigh your options and decide if taking this risk will be of optimum benefit for you. This is how a beginner's mind differs from an open mind. It is not that try everything for the sake of trying everything. But a beginner's mind recognizes that there is always room to learn, grow, and change. Becoming stuck and set in your ways is dangerous for your growth as a person, and in a society that is ever changing; you could find yourself getting left behind. Keep your beginner's mind while approaching all facets of life.

4. Trust

This attitude is not about trust in others so much as it is about trust in oneself. You alone know your heart, and you know how your emotions can affect you. Trust in yourself that you are the captain of your own ship. Remember, mindfulness is not about cutting off or repressing your emotions. They are important, and they shape you into who you are. Accept these emotions as a part of yourself, and trust in your own ability to govern them.

5. Non-Striving

Society claims that people should always be themselves, but compounds this with the insistence that you should conform with the best in order to be the best. You are you, and the person that you are is the best version of yourself. Mindfulness doesn't change you fundamentally; it just helps you understand that there was nothing needed to change in the first place. It brings out those best parts of you, in case it had been hidden away beneath stress, worry, and other negative emotions. Don't waste energy striving to be someone you aren't. Be yourself. And moreover, be happy with who 'yourself' is. Worrying about being something you're not is just as useless as worrying about things you can't change. Just as you are aware that all things happen in time for a reason, be aware that you are the person that you are for a reason.

6. Acceptance

Things are the way that they are, and they're going to happen the way they're going to happen. You can't stop it from happening, so don't lose any sleep over it. Accept that these things have happened, and move on. It is such a common thing amongst us, a part of human nature, to worry about changing things that we could not have changed. Learning to accept the world as it comes gives you the fortitude to deal with the bad news when it comes, but not to spend your whole life waiting for it. Life is life, and bumps in the road are going to come your way eventually. Accept it. It happens. Deal with it, and move on.

7. Letting Go

Like the useless trinkets you got rid of while cleaning, there are always going to be thoughts, emotions, and experiences that you don't want to let go of. Sometimes these emotions are negative, sometimes positive. Holding onto a positive emotion is fine, and can be helpful for giving you something to draw on in moments of severe stress. But holding to it too tightly is what causes a lot of the future uncertainty and unhappiness with the present. If you've become too attached to this positive memory, you become obsessed with looking to the past for a time when everything was better, and you want desperately to go back. Let that go. You cannot go back to the past, and wishing you could is causing your stress. Holding on to negative emotions happens when you fixate on a certain bad memory and continually think about it. It's in the past, it's done and it can't be changed. Let it go. At the other end of the spectrum, there are thoughts and emotions that you don't want to experience and actively avoid letting in your mind. Let go of the need to avoid certain things. Everything is going to happen anyway, so let everything happen.

If you want the word from the horse's mouth itself, the 7 Foundational Attitudes can also be found online. If you are the kind of person who really wants to practice this as though you were there in the program, print them off and stick them on your fridge. It's not quite like a checklist you can run through to decide you've successfully completed the program and eliminated stress and anxiety from your life. But it can serve as a reminder and a guide to keep you going.

Mindfulness-Based Stress Reduction is a tried and true method to deal with your worry, stress, and anxiety like no other. And while there is no height of mindfulness that you can reach, you can pass a milestone where your life and outlook has changed. Fear for the future and what it holds is a thing of the past.

Conclusion

In the end, everything is up to you. How much do you want to take up mindfulness? Do you even want to try it at all? There could still be something holding you back, wondering if this is the right way to deal with anxiety at all.

But if even the tiniest bit of you wants to try, follow that instinct. Even if your head is trying to be rational, telling you that it won't go anywhere and you won't manage to solve anything, try it anyway. Prove yourself wrong. Think of it as a challenge, if you have to. Don't you owe it to yourself to see if it will work out?

Mindfulness is deceptively complicated. It means different things to different people. You can be a mindful person, who doesn't really adhere to the practices but still incorporates the teachings into your everyday life. You can be a dedicated disciple of mindfulness, meditating every day and making each action with great deliberation. You can be an essentialist, in either form of the word.

Do you believe in the essence carried by all living things, being mindful of how it may impact your initial judgments of somebody? Or are you more of a modern essentialist, devoting yourself to the essentials of life, choosing quality over quantity? Either way, you are working to become the best possible version of yourself.

Unlike other spiritual practices or therapeutic exercises, mindfulness is not strenuous, nor does it require a great amount of work or study. It has a fairly low set of risks for a high reward, and those risks aren't anything that you can't prevent with a little foresight and knowledge.

After this book, no further learning is necessary. You know all that you need to know to bring mindfulness into your life. If it was suggested to you, but you didn't know if it was actually going to help, now you know. But you don't need somebody to tell you that you need it, it's in your own curiosity.

Looking out at the future is akin to staring down a dark, endless void. It's a long hallway with no door on the other side. It is a cliff face with no bridge to reach across the other side. For so many people, looking at this barren future is despairing. It's hopeless, there's no way out, it's never getting better than this, but those thoughts are only that—thoughts. You alone have the power to stop thinking about them. You're the one who gave them so much power over you in the first place. So stop letting these dark thoughts drive your soul. Take control of the steering wheel. Shine a light into the void. Cut a new doorway into the wall. Take a leap of faith and cross an unseen bridge.

Mindfulness can be so much more than just a way to calm down after a bad day. It is more than your new replacement of a stress ball. It can be an entirely new way to live. Free from doubts, from fear, from negativity. You can do it. You have all the tools you need. All it takes is a little time and a little training of the mind, and your journey into that bright, unseen future can begin. Happiness starts with a choice.

Jon Goldstein
Happiness starts with you.

www.ingramcontent.com/pod-product-compliance
Lightning Source LLC
Chambersburg PA
CBHW030116100526
44591CB00009B/420